THE
ROAD TO
GLORY

THE
ROAD TO
GLORY

Meditations on the Way from Here to Heaven

JUDGE THOMAS DILLON

WestBow
PRESS®
A DIVISION OF THOMAS NELSON
& ZONDERVAN

WestBow Press books may be ordered through booksellers or by contacting:

WestBow Press
A Division of Thomas Nelson & Zondervan
1663 Liberty Drive
Bloomington, IN 47403
www.westbowpress.com
1 (866) 928-1240

Scripture taken from the King James Version of the Bible.

This book is a work of non-fiction. Unless otherwise noted, the author and the publisher make no explicit guarantees as to the accuracy of the information contained in this book and in some cases, names of people and places have been altered to protect their privacy.

ISBN: 978-1-9736-4087-5 (sc)
ISBN: 978-1-9736-4088-2 (hc)
ISBN: 978-1-9736-2364-9 (e)

Library of Congress Control Number: 2018903437

Printed in the United States.

WestBow Press rev. date: 5/8/2018

I dedicate this book to my children, grandchildren, and great-grandchildren, intending it to be like a Gaelic solo on the pipes, each phrase of music repeated with a defining variation, a single theme—Christ crucified—repeated in each chapter.

CONTENTS

CHAPTER 1

ROAD OF LIGHT

When taking a trip, driving to a beautiful city to visit family and loved ones, how reassuring it is to see continuing road signs that explain the way and warn of dangers.

There is an eternal city where Christians who have passed away live, and, concerning it, this book contains a selection of foreshadows and illustrations in scripture. They are like road signs and explanatory maps of the way to the heavenly home of God's people. This home is "eternal and in the heavens."

We are created, as believers in Christ, to be very much alive in a resurrected body at Christ's return, like Christ's glorious body, forever (1 John 3:2). Those who are not Christians will also be somewhere forever. Jesus said, "These shall go away into everlasting punishment: but the righteous into life eternal" (Matt. 25:46). In the meantime, at the end of this life, our heavenly Father has a better city, where His Son, the Lord Jesus Christ, has prepared a place for His people. He said:

> In my Father's house are many mansions: If it were not so, I would have told you. I go to prepare a place for you. And if I go and prepare a place for you I will come again, and receive you unto myself; that where I am, there ye may be also. (John 14:2–3)

It is fascinating to view a description of a new home in this life, and fascinating it is to view our heavenly home, a city "eternal and in the heavens." This is described in Revelations 21:23–27:

> And the city had no need of the sun, neither of the moon, to shine in it: for the glory of God did lighten it, and the Lamb is the light thereof. And the nations of them which are saved shall walk in the light of it: and the kings of the earth do bring their glory and honour into it. And the gates of it shall not be shut at all by day: for there shall be no night there. And they shall bring the glory and honour of the nations into it. And there shall in no wise enter into it anything that defileth, neither whatsoever worketh abomination, or maketh a lie: but they which are written in the Lamb's book of life.

The road that leads to this glorious city is called the way of holiness:

> And an highway shall be there, and a way, and it shall be called The way of holiness; the unclean shall not pass over it; but it shall be for those: the

wayfaring men, though fools, shall not err therein. (Isa. 35:8)

The way to get on this road and stay on it, made plain, is the goal of this book.

So, let us look to this road. One of the first foreshadows on this theme that we shall look at took place the first time the scriptures mention God speaking. "And God said Let there be light: and there was light" (Gen. 1:3). Before God spoke these words many, many years ago, "the earth was without form and void; and darkness was upon the face of the deep." Then, at God's command, light shone on the earth.

This spectacular event, happening upon the establishment of our world, is set forth in the scriptures as a picture or foreshadow of a believer's conversion to Christ:

> For God who commanded the light to shine out of darkness, hath shined in our hearts, to give the light of the knowledge of the glory of God in the face of Jesus Christ. (2 Cor. 4:6)

Some find it difficult to understand that, just as this earth was void of life and without form and covered in darkness, so is one, spiritually, who does not know God. Often the temptation comes to compare one's life with one's friends in self-evaluation. The standard is otherwise. Jesus of Nazareth is the standard. Do our lives or any of us match the standard? He is the "true Light which lighteth every man that cometh into the world" (John 1:9). When we read of His life in the Gospels of the New

Testament, we see how, in our flesh, our lives do not in any way match up to His life. Jesus lived a life fulfilling God's law:

> Thou shalt love the Lord thy God with all thy heart, and with all thy soul, and with all thy strength, and with all thy mind; and thy neighbor as thyself. (Luke 10:27)

The penalty for disobedience: "the soul that sinneth, it shall die" (Ezek. 18:4). Among men, we see a sinless life—One—that lived out God's holy law absolutely. How is it that humankind can be blind to their own spiritual need while looking at Jesus?

In creation, immediately before the Lord spoke the words "let there be light," we read, "The Spirit of God moved upon the face of the waters" (Gen. 1:2).

So, when the Spirit of God moves on us, we see ourselves before God as we really are.

Isaiah, by tradition, the cousin of the king whose death he laments, more than seven hundred years before Christ, gives his testimony:

> In the year that King Uzziah died I saw also the Lord sitting upon a throne, high and lifted up, and his train filled the temple. Above it stood the seraphims: each one had six wings; with twain he covered his face, and with twain he covered his feet, and with twain he did fly. And one cried unto another, and said, Holy, holy, holy, is the Lord of hosts: the whole earth is full of his glory.

And the posts of the door moved at the voice of him that cried, and the house was filled with smoke. Then said I, Woe is me! for I am undone; because I am a man of unclean lips, and I dwell in the midst of a people of unclean lips: for mine eyes have seen the King, the Lord of hosts. (Isa. 6:1–5)

Peter, Christ's messenger, was a fisherman by trade. When Christ tells him to launch out into the deep and let down his nets for a draught, he replies:

Master, we have toiled all night, and have taken nothing; nevertheless, at thy word I will let down the net. And when they had this done, they inclosed a great multitude of fishes: and their net brake. And they beckoned unto their partners, which were in the other ship, that they should come and help them. And they came, and filled both the ships, so that they began to sink. When Simon Peter saw it, he fell down at Jesus' knees, saying, Depart from me; for I am a sinful man, O Lord. (Luke 5:5–8)

At the time of prayer, a publican, tax collector for the Roman government, sees in his mind Christ in the Jewish daily blood sacrifice as the mercy seat for his sin. With head bowed, he cries out as a sinner, asking the Lord Himself to take his place. "God, be merciful to me a sinner." This man went home justified (Luke 18:13–14). He not only had seen himself in the light of God—for he said of himself, "Me a sinner"—but he also saw the remedy. That is the mercy-seat propitiation whereupon was the sacrifice in the Old Testament worship, taking his place as a sinner because "the soul that sinneth, it shall die." Another, an innocent one, had taken his place, pointing to the sacrifice of Christ, our substitute on the cross yet to come. Now He has come.

The scriptures, including the passage below, clearly define the light that shines in our hearts. "The light of the glorious gospel of Christ." It is one of the very most important doctrines we can understand clearly. Thankfully, it is set forth in one sentence that is understandable and easily memorized. God's special messenger, Paul, tells us:

> For I delivered unto you, first of all, that which I also received; how that Christ died for our sins according to the scriptures; and that he was buried, and that he rose again the third day, according to the scriptures. (1 Cor. 15:3–4)

Anyone interested in forgiveness of sin and fellowship with God should memorize these verses and keep them fresh in mind. Why? Because the gospel is the power of God unto salvation to everyone who believes (Rom. 1:16).

So that an important principle of law could be remembered by young lawyers, a law professor at Harvard Law School made an assignment: From a given report of many pages, take the facts in the case, the law, and the conclusion, and put the operative facts, controlling law, and the conclusion into one sentence. This is called a "one-sentence brief." It is not an easy assignment. The Holy Spirit, in inspiration of the Bible, has done this to that most important principle: the glorious gospel of Christ. This one-sentence brief (1 Cor. 15:3–4) concerns the most important issue, because its message has eternal consequences for each of us.

God is light. Jesus said, "I am the light of the world." At God's command, the light of Christ crucified shines in our hearts. The Gospel of Mark begins with these words: "The beginning of the gospel of Jesus Christ, the Son of God." It is the shortest of the four Gospels, at only sixteen chapters long. But here in God's Word is a formula provided in one sentence, the essence, the very core of the gospel prophesied by the Old Testament prophets. It is pictured in the Jewish rituals and sacrificial system, and believed by Abraham, Jacob, Isaac, and thousands more of the Old Testament patriarchs.

We all know that we have broken the moral code of right and wrong. Yet, when hearing or reading the gospel, too often, the temptation comes to view it just as a philosophical concept, without taking it into our hearts in belief.

There is a darkness only God can dispel: spiritual darkness, compounded by notions and false religions. "But if thine eye be evil, thy whole body shall be full of darkness. If therefore the light that is in thee be darkness, how great is that darkness" (Matt. 6:23). Then, too, the gospel is foolishness to the mind full of pride; however, a person not "wise in his own conceits," a humble person, can and will accept it readily. As Jesus said to those full of religion and themselves, "the harlots go into the Kingdom of God before you" (Matt. 21:31). The Spirit of God "moved upon the face of the waters," before God spoke the light to shine on this earth; just so, the Spirit of God moves on the one who will believe and brings a willingness to receive the gospel: very needful because we are born into this world without the knowledge of the light of the glorious gospel.

Though all around be light, the blind person does not benefit from it. The light of the gospel has gone out like the sun shining on a clear day, but the blind still grope in the darkness of unbelief. The tragedy is that unbelief is intentional. Jesus said, "I am come a light into the world that whosoever believeth on me should not abide in darkness" (John 12:46).

It was not just a good man that died for our sins. It was the Christ, the Anointed One, God's Son. Jesus is the eternal Son of God. He was "in the beginning with God." The One, Jesus, whom wicked men nailed to a cross until he died was the Creator Himself. Had He been just a good man, we would have good reason to fear.

Jesus was a good man, but He was much more. He was and is God incarnate in the flesh, who died for our sins. He was and is the Christ, the Anointed One, God's only begotten Son. He was "in the beginning with God, all things were made by him and without him was not anything made that was made" (John 1:2–3).

What a revelation! The Jesus whom wicked men nailed to a cross, which He permitted them to do, was the Creator Himself! Had it been merely an ordinary human—even if, by our thinking, a very good one—who was crucified, we would have cause to doubt our justification by faith from our horrible sins. As we read in Psalm 49:7–9:

> None of them can by any means redeem his brother, nor give to God a ransom for him: (For the redemption of their soul is precious and it ceaseth forever:) That he should still live forever, and not see corruption.

Inasmuch as it was Jesus Christ who paid the penalty for our sins, He, the eternal Son of God Himself, "Who shall lay anything to the charge of God's elect? It is God that justifieth" (Rom. 8:33).

God raised Him from the dead the third day. His grave clothes that had wrapped Him were undisturbed, still in the form of His absent body when His disciples visited His tomb on the third day after His crucifixion; thus testifying to His disciples Peter and John, and testifying to us today. He arose (John 20:7–8). God accepted and accepts His sacrifice for our sins once and for all. God's Son, Jesus, is Lord and Christ, the living Savior. He is the light of the world; the light that shines in the darkness.

Paul tells us that Christ died "according to the Scriptures," and that He rose again "according to the Scriptures." The gospel is not something invented or brought out as a new thing. The truth and explanation of it are shown by years of prophecy beforehand. We shall look at some of these prophecies in future chapters. The benefits of the gospel in our relationships with God and others are enormous. We shall look at some of them.

One benefit is the enduring nature of the gospel light in our minds, once accepted. But the light and understanding of the truth depart if not acted on. On the other hand, if received, the light of truth continues in our hearts and minds, and we can walk in this light.

As Jesus said, "I am the light of the world; he that followeth me shall not walk in darkness, but shall have the light of life" (John 8:12).

Just as the moon and some of the stars hold and reflect the light of the sun, so it is with the believer. The night and the clouds may bring darkness to the earth, but above them the moon and the stars continue in their path in the light of the sun. And the one who believes and follows the risen Lord Jesus has continuing light; and does not walk in darkness, no matter, even in the "valley of the shadow of death." A cheering promise. "But if we walk in the light, as He is in the light, we have fellowship one with another, and the blood of Jesus Christ His son cleanseth us from all sin" (1 John 1:7).

When God created the earth He "divided the light from the darkness and God called the light day and the darkness he called night." Though we live in a land where the light of the gospel is all around us, we need not think it will always be so. In the time of the apostles, the gospel light shone on lands that now forbid the mention of Christ's Word. The darkness has followed the light, and our minds are such that when we hear the message of salvation by faith and do not look into it to understand it, soon we think on other things, and we close our minds to the word of truth. Jesus spoke to emphasize this danger: "When anyone heareth the Word of the Kingdom, and understandeth it not, then cometh the wicked one, and catcheth away that which was sown in his heart" (Matt. 13:19).

There is a difference between a road sign to a city on earth and a road sign to the heavenly city. The road sign to a city on earth stays right there even if ignored. Not so a road sign that leads to the heavenly city; such a sign comes to our heart and mind, and just because it is a spiritual light that flashes into the mind, it may not remain. Put differently, if not acted on, it goes away. (This is Satan, the devil, at work). The heart and mind then go back to spiritual darkness. Warning and examples abound in the scriptures. In Luke 15, when the starving prodigal son "came to himself," he said, "I will arise and go to my father." He didn't say, as many, in effect, do say, "I will return to my father later, at a more convenient time, when I have a decent appearance." Now is the time.

Lot's wife, fleeing from Sodom when warned of its immediate doom, looked back. Was it curiosity? Was it longing for the way of life left behind? In any event, she tarried, looked back, and met the judgment of Sodom. Fire and brimstone rained from above. Lot's wife was turned into a pillar of salt (Gen. 19:26).

Is the light of the gospel in your heart and mind? Be pleased to keep it and continue believing in Christ. If forsaken, the light will go, and darkness will come to stay.

To illustrate: A fisherman hired a boat with a three-man crew for sport fishing and put out to sea from a harbor on the shore of eastern Mexico. It was a beautiful day with a blue sky and no hint of the grim events that were to follow.

Large barracuda struck the fisherman's lure, one after another, as the boat trolled through a calm sea. One of the crew took the fish off the line when pulled in. Another crew member cleaned and packed the fish in barrels containing pickles, onions, lemons, and tomatoes; the fish to be preserved for winter food in the little village where the crew lived in the woods. After just an hour in this mixture, the barracuda were delicious.

Then, a warning sign appeared out of the south: the horizon grew black, cleft repeatedly with red flashes of lightning. The crew quickly stowed the fishing gear. They covered the vats of pickled fish with a tarp and roped them together. And then they made a big mistake.

The crew member at the boat controls tried to outrun the storm by heading east, away from land. Moments later, smoke billowed from the diesel engine that powered the boat. It burned until the boat lost power and quit.

Then, the storm broke upon the little boat and its crew, immersing them in total darkness, a blanket of rain, and howling wind. The storm anchor kept the boat from being swamped, but the waves still crashed in on the deck. The four men huddled in the cabin of the boat.

Minutes passed. The fierceness of the storm passed, but the sea was heavy, with large, rolling waves, and the sky was overcast. A heavy mist and light rain covered the water. The boat was without power, lying dead in the water.

The crew tried to use the ship-to-shore radio, but without success. The distance of the boat from the port, after trying to outrun the storm, was greater than the range of the radio. Now the boat and crew were lost at sea, with no power to move the boat and no way to contact port or to secure help.

There was nothing for the crew to do—they were helpless. All had become discouraged, when a small burst of blue sky came overhead. The rain stopped for a few moments. A beautiful sight appeared. About two hundred yards portside, ploughing through the rolling waves, was a huge gray freighter. The crew leader radioed the freighter. The freighter relayed the position and circumstance to shore. Help was on its way. And then, just as suddenly as it had appeared, the gray freighter disappeared into the mist.

This story depicts the lostness of a person without God in this world. The attempt to outrun the storms of life is futile. The light of the gospel comes like a ship of rescue, and, if not believed in, it will disappear like a ship in the mist.

The darkness of the natural mind in man needs no argument to prove. History, with its testimony of murders, hatred, and foolish religions, affirms it. Now we have the fullness of light in

His coming and dying and being raised from the dead; it gives recovery of life to all who believe.

He, coming into the world, lights every human being that ever has lived, lives now, or ever will live (John 1:9). Adam, the first man, is not the head of the human race. Jesus, who always was, who is now, and who always will be, is that head. His life is not merely the plumb line, the standard, that shows what we ought to be—He is more. He is the ransom for all mankind: "for there is one God, and one mediator between God and men, the man Christ Jesus; Who gave himself a ransom for all, to be testified in due time" (1 Tim. 2:5–6). Does that mean that all people will be saved from their sins? Certainly not. Jesus said, "These shall go away into everlasting punishment: but the righteous into life eternal." In what way, then, is Jesus the Savior of all mankind, as the scripture says?

Like Adam, the first man, we all die. But in Christ shall all be made alive:

> But now is Christ risen from the dead, and become the first fruits of them that sleep. For since by man came death, by man came also the resurrection of the dead. For as in Adam all die, even so in Christ shall all be made alive. But every man in his own order: Christ the first fruits; afterward they that are Christ's at his coming. Then cometh the end, when he shall have delivered up the kingdom to God, even the Father; when he shall have put down all rule and all authority and power. (1 Cor. 15:20–24)

So, then, we all will be made alive, but at different times. Everyone who has ever lived will be raised from the grave with a body that cannot die. An eternal body. Death, the last enemy, is and will be conquered by Christ. No one is accountable to God for having a sinful nature; and all of us have a sinful nature.

In that way, Jesus is Savior of all. Jesus is the Lamb of God that taketh away the sin of the world. "The next day John seeth Jesus coming unto him, and saith, Behold the Lamb of God, which taketh away the sin of the world" (John 1:29). The word *sin* is singular. It speaks of that which we had upon coming into this world at birth. All infants who die are, therefore, eternally saved.

Jesus died for the sins (plural) only of believers. Unbelievers are accountable for their sins. We who have received the resurrected Christ, by faith, in payment for our sins, by God's grace are not accountable. The awful price in judgment has been paid for us by Christ on the cross.

John, Christ's personal friend and special messenger, writes of the bodily resurrection of those who have not received Christ during their lives on earth:

> And I saw the great white throne, and him that sat on it, from whose face the earth and the heaven fled away; and there was found no place for them. And I saw the dead, small and great, stand before God; and the books were opened; and another book was opened, which is the book of life; and the dead were

judged out of those things which were written in the books according to their works. And the sea gave up the dead which were in it; and death and hell delivered up the dead which were in them; and they were judged every man according to their works. And death and hell were cast into the lake of fire. This is the second death. And whosoever was not found written in the book of life was cast into the lake of fire. (Rev. 20:11–15)

The question, yes, the burning issue is: are you—am I—in Christ's book of life? "Verily, verily, I say unto you, He that heareth my word, and believeth on him that sent me, hath everlasting life, and shall not come into condemnation: but is passed from death unto life" (John 5:24).

The road to heaven? The Lord Jesus Christ alone! He is "the way, the truth and the life." He said "no one goes to the Father but by me." How to get on that road? Faith alone! Believe in the Lord Jesus Christ. How to stay on that road? Faith alone! We walk by faith and not by sight.

CHAPTER 2

THE SERPENT IN THE WAY

On the sixth day of creation, the Lord formed mankind, Adam and Eve, and placed them in a garden of paradise. He gave one command, saying, "Of every tree of the garden thou mayest freely eat: but of the tree of the knowledge of good and evil, thou shalt not eat of it: for in the day that thou eatest thereof thou shalt surely die" (Gen. 2:16–17).

Thereafter, temptation came to the woman, Eve, by one the scriptures call the serpent. This is the description of the serpent: "Now the serpent was more subtle than any beast in the field which the Lord God had made. And he said to the woman, Yeah, hath God said, Ye shall not eat of every tree in the garden?" (Gen. 3:1).

Agnostics have bemused themselves about this serpent that talked, as serpents do not have a voice box. I have had an expensive sports car, which I didn't need, talk to me through a plate-glass window, and that car didn't even have a mouth. The conversation went something like this: Upon my admiring the beauty of the car in the window at its location, it said, in effect: "You have worked hard. You deserve the fruits of your labor. So, why don't you come in and see a salesman about a test-drive?" Agnostics can't see the truth through the cloud of their own pride. Their bias is amazing. The serpent *did* speak to the mind of Eve.

The real speaker to the woman was "that old serpent, called the Devil, and Satan, which deceiveth the whole world" (Rev. 12:9).

Satan used the serpent—a beautiful beast at that time—as a point of communication. How he has access to our minds is a mystery, but he does, and in words most interesting, much like a master salesman, he draws Eve into conversation by making an obviously incorrect charge against the Lord. She hastens to correct this, and lays herself open to deception: "the serpent was more subtle than any beast of the field." The scripture, on occasion, calls a person by the name of an animal that his or her character resembles. Jesus, for example, speaking of King Herod said, "Go ye, and tell that fox" (Luke 13:32).

We can learn of the character of the tempter and his way by the example of the serpent. A serpent takes its prey for food with much more craft and guile than other creatures. The lion is a hunter and takes its food, but with much exertion and danger. This is true of other beasts of prey. It is true even of man, and many have died struggling for a living. Not so the serpent. It takes on a perfect camouflage, and waits unseen and unexpected in a place where its prey will be found. Then, it strikes, killing its prey with the poison in its fangs, or folding and coiling itself around its prey to suffocate it.

So, we have to do not with an ordinary snake tempting Eve, but with Satan, the devil—a cunning and evil spirit, a snakelike spirit. Satan has an unseen pathway to our minds. As will be seen, he can speak in words not only understandable but also most appealing in their deceitfulness. His bite is poisonous.

We know that the Lord made the heavens and the earth and all the creatures; but, surely, He didn't make such a creature as Satan! He didn't. We can see from the scriptures from whence comes this evil spirit. The Lord God created him as Lucifer, son of the morning, one of God's most powerful angels. He, from that high position, became an enemy of God because of pride in himself. Here is the record:

> "How are thou fallen from heaven, O Lucifer, son of the morning! How are thou cut down to the ground, which didst weaken the nations! For thou has said in thine heart, I will exalt my throne above the stars of God: I will sit also upon the mount of the congregation, in the sides of the north: I will ascend above the heights of the clouds; I will be like the most High. Yet thou shalt be brought down to hell, to the sides of the pit." (Isa. 14:12–15)

He came to tempt the woman, not as the devil—which he was—but, rather, camouflaged as a bringer of light and benefit. Yet the mark of evil is on him, because he began by questioning God's goodness, misquoting God's Word. The Lord's warning was absolute concerning the tree of the knowledge of good and evil: "Ye shall not eat thereof; The day that thou eatest thereof thou shalt surely die." The woman's defense to the tempter was quite mistaken. She "said unto the serpent, we may eat of the fruit of the trees of the garden, but the fruit which is in the midst of the garden, God hath said, ye shall not eat of it, neither shall ye touch it, lest ye die" (Gen. 3:2–3). This defense erred in at least two ways.

The Lord had made no prohibition against touching the fruit. To include this, as prohibited, was a dangerous decoy. The man and woman could touch the fruit without penalty. Thus, they could conclude eating the fruit would not bring penalty either—a fatal conclusion.

The woman's statement, in misquoting the Lord, saying, "lest ye die" was a fatal presumption. His warning was "ye shall surely die."

This same mistake is often made; God's warning "the soul that sinneth, it shall die" (Ezek. 18:4), is changed to something like "the soul that sinneth might even die." Thus, the fear of the Lord is turned from our hearts.

It is doubtful that the woman should have even had a conversation with the tempter at all after he had maligned God in his opening question. However, had she known God's Word and believed it as a defense, she would have been safe. Note how the Lord Jesus used the Word to gain victory over temptation to use his miraculous power to win benefit: "And the devil said unto him, If thou be the Son of God, command this stone that it be made bread. And Jesus answered him saying, It is written, That man shall not live by bread alone, but by every word of God" (Luke 4:3–4). And on the two following temptations, to use his power for his own benefit, which he never did, He refuted Satan with scriptures.

In the woman's case, upon seeing either her mistake or her disregard of God's Word, Satan pressed his advantage, and the serpent said unto the woman:

> "Ye shall not surely die: For God doth know that in the day ye eat thereof, then your eyes shall be opened, and ye shall be as gods, knowing good and evil." And when the woman saw that the tree was good for food, and that it was pleasant to the eyes, and a tree to be desired to make one, she took of the fruit thereof, and did eat, and gave also unto her husband with her; and he did eat. And the eyes of them both were opened, and they knew that they were naked; and they sewed fig leaves together, and made themselves aprons. (Gen. 3:4-7)

The woman chose to believe the serpent rather than even her own mistaken quotation of God's Word. This is the heart of the tragedy. What one believes dictates what one does.

If some rite or ritual is thought to be necessary for us to be acceptable to God, then faith is insufficient. Paul, the Lord's special messenger (an apostle) warns, "But I fear, lest by any means, as the serpent beguiled Eve through his subtlety, so your minds should be corrupted from the simplicity that is Christ" (2 Cor. 11:3). The argument is the same, whatever the "something else" is. Examples abound: "be baptized, or pray the right prayer"; "join the right church"; "keep the law of Moses"; etc., etc. I am not putting down the value of the ordinances of baptism and the Lord's Supper, nor am I speaking ill of the power and importance of prayer, which have nothing to do with being justified by God and receiving eternal life, important as they are. The Holy Scriptures are clear and plain. "And if by grace, then is it no more of works: otherwise grace is no more grace. But if it be of works, then is it no more grace: otherwise work is no more work" (Rom. 11:6). This theme is so important that it is repeated many times in the scriptures, in different circumstances and different times, by types and symbols, by illustration and warning.

To the doubter, one can say, in effect, "Surely, you can credit God's only begotten Son, Jesus, with knowing the right way." On this issue, Jesus had an interesting encounter with a Jewish master rabbi who knew much of the scriptures but didn't understand the most important way of eternal salvation and entrance into the kingdom of God. Here is the record:

> There was a man of the Pharisees named Nicodemus, a ruler of the Jews: The same came to Jesus by night, and said unto him, "Rabbi, we know that thou art a teacher come from God: for no man can do these

miracles that though doest except God be with him." Jesus answered and said unto him, "Verily, verily, I say unto thee, Except a man be born again, he cannot see the kingdom of God." Nicodemus saith unto him, "How can a man be born when he is old? Can he enter the second time into his mother's womb and be born?" Jesus answered, "Verily, verily, I say unto thee, Except a man be born of water and of the Spirit, he cannot enter the kingdom of God. That which is born of the flesh is flesh; and that which is born of the Spirit is spirit. Marvel not that I said unto thee, Ye must be born again. The wind bloweth where it listeth, and thou hearest sound thereof, but canst not tell whence it cometh, and whither it goeth: so is everyone that is born of the Spirit." Nicodemus answered and said unto him, "How can these things be?" Jesus answered and said unto him, "Art thou a master of Israel, and knowest not these things? Verily, verily, I say unto thee, We speak that we do know, and testify that we have seen; and ye receive not our witness. If I have told you earthly things and ye believe not, how shall ye believe, if I tell you of heavenly things? And no man ascendeth up to heaven, but he that came down from heaven, even the Son of man which is in heaven. And as Moses lifted up the serpent in the wilderness, even so must the Son of man be lifted up: That whosoever believeth in him should not perish, but have eternal life." (John 3:1–15)

The event, when Moses lifted up the serpent of brass, was familiar to Nicodemus. It is recorded in Numbers 21:4–9:

And they journeyed from Mount Hor by way of the Red Sea, to compass the land of Edom: and the soul of the people was much discouraged because of the way. And the people spake against God, and against Moses, "Wherefore, have ye brought us up out of Egypt to die in the wilderness? for there is no bread, neither is there any water; and our soul loatheth this light bread." And the Lord sent fiery serpents among the people, and they bit the people; and much people of Israel died. Therefore the people came to Moses, and said, "We have sinned, for we have spoken against the Lord, and against thee; pray unto the Lord, that he take away the serpents from us." And Moses prayed for the people. And the Lord said unto Moses, "Make thee a fiery serpent, and set it upon a pole: and it shall come to pass, that everyone that is bitten, when he looketh upon it, shall live." And Moses made a serpent of brass, and put it upon a pole, and it came to pass that if a serpent had bitten any man, when he beheld the serpent of brass, he lived.

Of course, the serpent of brass on the pole represented Christ "who was made to be sin" for us lifted up on a Roman cross: "that we might be made the righteousness of God in him" (2 Cor. 5:21). Christ crucified draws people unto Him. There are interesting points in this comparison, as seen above: "And as Moses lifted up the serpent in the wilderness, even so must the Son of a man be lifted up."

The dying people of Israel were to look at the serpent of brass. Sinners—that includes all of us—are to look on Christ crucified. Here, looking is given as a definition of saving faith. Jesus went on to say "that whosoever believeth in him should not perish, but have eternal life."

God said to look at the serpent of brass lifted up on a pole, and nothing else. This look of faith alone was all that God required of the sinners to heal from the serpent's bite. Looking required believing. Doubtless, many who were bitten did not look. The ones who did not look died from the snake bites, as a result of their unbelief.

The healing was for all who would look on the brass serpent. It was freely given. So is the work of Christ in salvation: it is free for all who will look on His finished work on the cross and His resurrection. The invitation to salvation from the deadly bite of sin is to "whosoever believeth in him." All of Israel that looked on the serpent of brass were healed. Just so, all who truly believe in Christ have everlasting life instead of everlasting death. As Jesus promised, so it is.

The cure of the serpent's bite by simply looking on a serpent made of brass lifted upon a pole was miraculous. The power for the healing came from God. There is no medical or rational explanation. So, when one believes in Christ, the new life in Christ that comes to such a one is miraculous. It is the work of God. This is what Jesus meant in talking to Nicodemus and saying "ye must be born again."

The serpent lifted up for Israel was for a limited time. We read in the account in verse 10, "the children of Israel set forward." The time for healing was over. So it is that the time of salvation is limited. Now is the day of salvation: "For he saith, I have heard thee in a time accepted, and in the day of salvation have

I succoured thee: behold, now is the accepted time; behold, now is the day of salvation" (2 Cor. 6:2).

The evangelist D. L. Moody gives this account of his experience with an American Civil War soldier who, wounded on the battlefield, lay dying:

> And I said, "I would take you right up in my arms and carry you into the kingdom of God, if I could, but I cannot do it. I cannot help you die!"
>
> "Who can?" he asked.
>
> "The Lord Jesus Christ can – He came for that purpose."
>
> He shook his head and said: "He cannot save me. I have sinned all my life."
>
> "But He came to save sinners," I replied. I thought of his mother in the North and I was sure that she was anxious that he should die in peace; so I resolved I would stay with him. I prayed two or three times and repeated all the promises I could; for it was evident that in a few hours he would be gone.
>
> I said I wanted to read him a conversation that Christ had with a man who was anxious about his soul. I turned to the third chapter of John. His eyes were riveted on me; and when I came to the fourteenth and fifteenth verses he caught up the words, "As Moses lifted up the serpent in the wilderness, even so must the Son of man be lifted up: that whosoever

believeth in him should not perish but have eternal life."

He stopped me and said: "Is that there?" I answered yes, and he asked me to read it again; and I did so. He leaned his elbows on the cot and clasping his hands together, said, "That's good; won't you read it again?" I read it the third time and then went on with the rest of the chapter.

When I had finished, his eyes were closed, his hands were folded, and there was a smile on his face. Oh, how it was lit up! What a change had come over it! I saw his lips quivering, and leaning over him, I heard in a faint whisper, "As Moses lifted up the serpent in the wilderness, even so must the Son of man be lifted up; that whosoever believeth in him should not perish, but have eternal life." He opened his eyes and said, "That's enough; don't read any more." He lingered a few hours, pillowing his head on those two verses and then went up in one of Christ's chariots, to take his seat in the kingdom of God.[1]

---

[1] James S. Bell, Jr., *The D. L. Moody Collection* (Chicago: Moody Press, 1997), 133. Used with permission of the publisher.

CHAPTER 3

CLOTHED FOR
THE TRIP

Like awakening from a bad dream and finding it reality, our first parents, upon eating the forbidden fruit, see they are naked. They make aprons by fastening fig leaves together, certainly not a satisfactory covering; in fact, one subject to falling off at a touch and breaking up as it dries.

They hear the voice of the Lord walking the garden. It is a time of fellowship with the Lord in the cool of the day. Fear takes hold of Adam and Eve. They hide themselves in the bushes (Gen. 3:7–8).

They hide themselves from God in vain, like a small infant who covers its eyes and thinks no one can see it. The Lord knew where they hid. He knows where we hide. And, just as Adam and Eve tried a covering of fig leaves, today, mankind works at a covering, though with the experience of the ages, the covering has developed more varieties—including drugs, alcohol, and sometimes religious works—but is always self-righteousness.

The Lord says, in speaking to our first parents, "Adam, where are thou?" His call is not so that He can find Adam, but, rather, so Adam can find the Lord. The Lord knows where people are today— each and every one. It was after the prodigal son, in misery, came to himself, that he said, "I will arise and go to my father" (Luke 15:18).

We will give particular attention to the call of Adam. In it we see the Lord Jesus Christ come to "seek and save that which is lost." The Trinity—Father, Son, and Holy Spirit—all participate in the creation and redemption of mankind. Nevertheless, the work of creation and redemption are particularly the work of the Son of God, whom we know as the Lord Jesus Christ, as is shown in the scriptures:

> For by him were all things created that are in heaven, and that are in earth, visible and invisible, whether they be thrones, or dominions, or principalities, or powers: all things were created by him, and for him: And he is before all things, and by him all things consist. And he is the head of the body, the church: who is the beginning, the firstborn from the dead; that in all things he might have preeminence. For it pleased the Father that in him should all fullness dwell. (Col. 1:16–19)

And we also read, "All things were made by him; and without him was not anything made that was made. In him was life;

and the life was the light of men" (John 1:3–4). These verses speak of Jesus, the living Word of God who "was made flesh and dwelt among us" (John 1:14). He says in Proverbs 8:31, "Rejoicing in the habitable part of his earth; and my delights were with the sons of men."

When Adam and Eve hear the voice of the Lord walking in the garden, it is none other than the Son of God, Jesus, the Lord of glory. His call led, as we shall later see, to faith, to life instead of death—the latter brought upon themselves through their own disobedience. God calls today with the same purpose in mind: to seek and save that which was lost (Luke 19:10). He called the treasurer of Ethiopia by placing an evangelist, Philip, in his company to explain the gospel while the Ethiopian was returning home from Jerusalem. The Holy Spirit of God gave the Ethiopian an open and seeking mind. Upon hearing the truth, he confesses, "I believe that Jesus Christ is the Son of God" (Acts 8:37).

He called a Philippian jailer through the songs of praise to God by inmates Paul and Silas, who were locked up for preaching the gospel. The Lord gave further credit to His call by shaking the earth so that the doors of the jail were opened.

Then, seeking to kill himself for the loss of his prisoners, the jailer attempted suicide with a sword. Seeing him, Paul cried, "do thyself no harm for we are all here." The jailer fell down before Paul and Silas, saying, "Sirs what must I do to be saved?" The answer: "believe on the Lord Jesus Christ and thou shalt be saved and thy house." Believing, the jailer took them to his house, washed the wounds of Paul and Silas, fed them, and rejoiced, believing in God with all his house (Acts 16:25–34).

Adam explains to the Lord why he hid in the garden: "I was naked." His efforts to cover his nakedness were worthless, even to himself, in the presence of God. Fig leaves make poor clothing, even in hiding. We are reminded of our own attempts when we try to use our good works to cover our failures. "Our righteousness's are as filthy rags" (Isa. 64:6). God's redeemed ones in heaven are clothed in white (Rev. 7:9). God granted Adam repentance from his foolishness. Thankfully, He has granted some of us the same.

The record in Genesis 3:11–15 is fascinating. The Lord asks Adam, "Has thou eaten of the tree whereof I commanded thee that thou should not eat?" Adam responds, "The woman whom thou gavest to be with me, she gave me of the tree, and I did eat." The Lord then turns to Eve:

> And the Lord God said unto the woman, "What is this that thou has done?" And the woman said, "The serpent beguiled me, and I did eat." And the Lord God said unto the serpent, "Because thou hast done this, thou art cursed above all cattle, and above every beast of the field; upon thy belly shalt thou go, and dust shalt thou eat all the days of thy life: And I will put enmity between thee and the woman, and between thy seed and her seed; it shall bruise thy head, and thou shalt bruise his heel."

Adam confesses his sin by blaming his wife, saying, "the woman thou gavest me"; he even blames the Lord Himself.

In so doing, he shows how futile a mere confession of sins is to an unbeliever. An unconverted sinner, Adam needed to repent, change his mind about himself and the way of salvation, with repentance toward God and faith toward the Lord Jesus Christ. God responded to the self-righteous confessions of sin in judgment. Unto the woman He said, "I will greatly multiply thy sorrow and thy conception; in sorrow thou shalt bring forth children; and thy desire shall be thy husband, and he shall rule over thee" (Gen. 3:16). And to the man, He said:

> "Because thou has hearkened unto the voice of thy wife, and has eaten of the tree, of which I commanded thee, saying, Thou shalt not eat of it: cursed is the ground for thy sake; in sorrow shalt thou eat of it all the days of thy life; Thorns and thistles shall it bring forth to thee; and thou shalt eat the herb of the field; In the sweat of thy face shalt thou eat bread, till thou return unto the ground; for out of it was thou taken: for dust thou art and unto dust shalt thou return." (Gen. 3:17–19)

The Lord also sentenced the serpent, and, in so doing, He made a wonderful promise: "And I will put enmity between thee and the woman, and between thy seed and her seed; it shall bruise thy head, and thou shalt bruise his heel" (Gen. 3:15). Here is the first promise to you and me and all men everywhere—not to just Adam and Eve—of victory over our tempter and destroyer, Satan, the devil and destroyer.

The Seed of the woman is Jesus. All others of mankind descending from Adam have their beginning in the seed of a man. The exception is Jesus, the Christ, who was like sinful flesh but was not sinful flesh, so that He could carry our sins in His own body on the cross. Thus, we see how God protects the virgin birth of Jesus. He was conceived by the Holy Spirit, without a human father, in the body of Mary, the blessed virgin (Matt. 1:18; Luke 1:34–35).

Satan brought death to mankind. He still brings death, eternal death. It was death that Jesus, the Seed of the woman, conquered. He is the firstfruits, the beginning of the resurrection. He will bring resurrection to every person ever born, in due time:

> But now is Christ risen from the dead, and become the first fruits of them that slept. For since by man came death, by man came also the resurrection of the dead. For as in Adam all die, even so in Christ shall all be made alive. But every man in his own order: Christ the firstfruits; afterward they that are Christ's at his coming. Then cometh the end, when he shall have delivered up the kingdom to God, even the Father; when he shall have put down all rule and all authority and power. For he must reign, till he hath put all enemies under his feet. (1 Cor. 15:20–25)

The resurrection by faith of those who are "in Christ" is called the first resurrection and precedes the resurrection of the wicked (Rev. 20:5). The Lord Jesus Christ will return, fulfilling the promise of his righteous and complete reign on this earth—a time of peace and prosperity. Following is the resurrection of the wicked, and their judgment:

> And I saw the dead, small and great, stand before God; and the books were opened: and another book

was opened, which is the book of life: and the dead were judged out of those things which were written in the books, according to their works. And the sea gave up the dead which were in it; and death and hell delivered up the dead which were in them: and they were judged every man according to their works. And death and hell were cast into the lake of fire. This is the second death. And whosoever was not found written in the book of life was cast into the lake of fire. (Rev. 20:12–15)

Those wonderful events, yet to come, will fulfill that promise the Seed of the woman (Christ) "shall bruise the head of the serpent."

The devil bruised Christ's heel in that he stirred up wicked men to crucify him. Christ rose from the dead with open victory. He is the "first fruits of the resurrection." The harvest is yet to come. In the meantime, the Lord commands men everywhere to repent (Acts 17:30).

Following the Lord's promise of grace and victory over death, He pronounced judgments on mankind—man and woman. While He was pronouncing judgments, a miracle was taking place. His precious promise was germinating toward spiritual eternal life in the heart of Adam, like seed growing in fertile ground. The benefits of His promised Seed were starting to manifest, then and there.

Instead of bemoaning his fate resulting from judgments of toil, sweat, and thorns, Adam comes forth with a joyful confession of faith in the naming of his wife and his reason for doing so. She who had been "The woman whom thou gavest to be with me, she gave me of the tree and I did eat," is now "Eve," meaning life. Why? Because she is the mother of living (or life giver). Remember—Adam was not looking from our point of view, knowing the millions of the woman's descendants. There were no other people. One was promised to the couple. Adam and Eve had suffered spiritual death and were dying physically by believing the serpent. "Thou shalt surely die" had come on them. Now the promise of the coming Seed had opened Adam's mind with a God-given faith. The Promised One would bring life at the expense of Himself. Considering his circumstances, Adam's understanding and faith constitute a miracle.

What does the Lord do upon Adam's confession of faith, calling his wife Eve (life) because she was the mother of the life (Christ)? He "makes coats of skins and clothed them." This clothing was not a little loin covering, such as what they had themselves made with fig leaves. Man, in natural pride, imagines he is only a sinner in part and needs only some of his acts forgiven, whereas the truth about mankind is that in his flesh, there is no good thing:

> Being filled with all unrighteousness, fornication, wickedness, covetousness; maliciousness; full of envy, murder, debate, deceit, malignity; whisperers, backbiters, haters of God, despiteful, proud, boasters, inventors of evil things, disobedient to parents, Without understanding, covenant breakers, without natural affection, implacable, unmerciful: Who knowing the judgment of God, that they which commit such things are worthy of death, not

only do the same, but have pleasure in them that do them. (Rom. 1:29–32)

The Lord clothed them entirely. Since the Lord made it, no doubt it was elegant and beautiful.

We see remnants of man's early clothing at a later date, in the discovery of the so-called ice man found in 1991, in a glacier in the European Alps. This discovery astounded and contradicted many of the beliefs of archeologists. Radio-carbon dated at 3300 BC, he had been neatly attired in a beautiful fur robe sewn from ibex chamois and deer skin. His attire and weaponry showed he was far advanced form the popular conception of the caveman or a citizen of what is thought to be primitive Neolithic culture. The *Encyclopaedia Britannica* has further interesting data. This reinforces our belief that Adam and Eve were not created or clothed as simple groping savages. The human race has, in part, degenerated into such, not advanced from such.

The death of the animal at the Lord's hand for skins covering the nakedness of our first parent's points ahead to the great event when Christ died. The Seed of the woman, the Lord Jesus Christ, becomes our covering from sin, and, in His resurrection, He gives justification and life.

Jesus spoke of the door and the road to life:

> "Enter ye in at the strait gate: for wide is the gate, and broad is the way, that leadeth to destruction, and many there be which go in thereat: Because strait is

the gate, and narrow is the way, which leadeth unto life, and few there be that find it." (Matt. 7:13–14)

Picture a wide, flat expanse. It is crowded with people rushing like lemmings to the edge of a cliff; then, a press over by the crowd behind, to death. But en route, on the right side of the expanse, is a wall of granite. In that wall there is a door. A few people go in the door to a narrow way and find, not destruction but everlasting life.

Adam entered in at the door, the "straight gate and the narrow way." And the record shows he went in without works, but by faith alone.

The record of Adam's miraculous faith shows another important principle. Adam didn't try to reform his life. He didn't make vows. He didn't bow in worship. He didn't give gifts. He didn't pray. All he did was believe the gospel: the promise of the coming Seed of the woman. It has been now fulfilled in Christ: His death for our sins and resurrection for our righteousness.

Adam looked at God's promise as a certainty. Naming his wife "Life," he entered into life—or, rather, life entered him. God's promise was not a dim look to the future but, in his mind, a fact of reality. And, when the New Testament uses the word *hope*, it has assurance tied to it like a promissory note from God for eternal life (Heb. 11:1). And now, Christ, the Seed of the woman, has bruised the head of the serpent. Now is the accepted time to claim the benefit. As James Denney says:

The work of reconciliation, in the sense of the New Testament, is a work which is finished, and which we must conceive to be finished, before the gospel is preached. It is the good tidings of the Gospel, with which the evangelists go forth, that God has wrought in Christ a work of reconciliation which avails for no less than the world, and of which the whole world may have the benefit. The summons of the evangelist is – 'Receive the reconciliation; consent that it become effective in your case.' The work of reconciliation is not a work wrought upon the souls of men, though it is a work wrought in their interests, and bearing so directly upon them that we can say God has reconciled the world to Himself; it is a work – as Cromwell said of the covenant – outside of us, in which God so deals in Christ with the sin of the world, that it shall no longer be a barrier between Himself and men.[2]

But, still, our ancient foe, Satan, who bruised Christ's heel, but now crucified and crushed forever, would keep us from this precious promise now fulfilled, like a head-crushed snake that can still strike.

Luther puts it plainly:

Let us receive this most sweet doctrine, so full of comfort, with thanksgiving, and with an assured faith, which teacheth that Christ being made a curse for us (that is a sinner under the wrath of God) did put upon Himself our person, and laid our sins upon His own shoulders, saying, I have committed the sins which all men have committed.

---

[2] James Denney, DD, *The Death of Christ* (Minneapolis: Klock & Klock Christian Publishers, 1982), 103–104. (Originally published by Hodder & Stroughton, London, England 1911.)

Therefore He was made a curse indeed according to the law, not for Himself, but, as Paul saith, for us. For unless He had taken upon Himself my sins and thine, and the sins of the whole world, the law had had no right over Him, for it condemneth none but sinners only, and holdeth them under the curse. Wherefore, He could neither have been a curse, or die, since the only cause of the curse and of death is sin, from which He was free. But because He had taken upon Himself our sins, not by constraint, but of His own good will, it behooved Him to bear the punishment, and wrath of God: not for His own person, but for our person.

So, making a happy change with us, He took upon Him our sinful person, and gave unto us His innocent and victorious person; wherewith we, being now clothed, are freed from the curse of the law. For Christ was willingly made a curse for us, saying, "As touching My own person, I am blessed and need nothing. But I will abase Myself and put upon Me your person" (Phil. 2:7); that is to say, your human nature, and I will walk in the same among you, and will suffer death, to deliver you from death. Now, He thus bearing the sin of the whole world in our person, was taken, suffered, was crucified and put to death, and became a curse for us. But because He was a person divine and everlasting, it was impossible that death should hold Him. Wherefore He arose again the third day from the dead, and now living for ever: and there is neither sin nor death found in Him anymore, but only righteousness, life and everlasting blessedness. This image and this mirror we must have continually before us, and behold the same with a steadfast eye of faith. He that doth so, hath this innocency and victory of Christ,

although he be never so great a sinner. By faith
only therefore we are made righteousness, for faith
layeth hold of this innocency and victory in Christ.
Look then how much thou believest this, so much
doest thou enjoy it. If thou believe sin, death, and
the curse to be abolished, they are abolished. For
Christ hath overcome and taken away these unto
Himself, and will have us to believe, that like as in
His own person, there is now no sin or death, even
so there is none in ours, seeing He has performed
and accomplished all things for us.

Wherefore if sin vex thee, and death terrify thee,
think that it is (as indeed it is) but an imagination,
and a false illusion of the devil. For in very deed
there is now no sin, no curse, no death, no devil, to
hurt us anymore, for Christ hath vanquished and
abolished all these things. The victory of Christ
is most certain, and there is no defect in the thing
itself, but in our incredulity; for to reason it is a hard
matter to believe these inestimable good things, and
unspeakable riches. Moreover, Satan, with his fiery
darts, and his ministers, with their wicked and false
doctrine, go about to wrest from us, and utterly to
deface this doctrine: and specially for this article
which we so diligently teach, we sustain the hatred
and cruel persecution of Satan, and of the world; for
Satan feeleth the power and fruit of this article."[3]

---

[3] Martin Luther, *Commentary on Galatians* (Grand Rapids, MI: Kregel
Classics, an imprint of Kregel Publications, 1979), 171–73. (A reprint of
the 1850 edition published by the Harrison Trust, London, under the title
A Commentary on St. Paul's Epistle to the Galatians.)

CHAPTER 4

THE WRONG WAY ON THE RIGHT ROAD

"I have gotten a man from the Lord," Adam's wife, Eve, said. No doubt, in the depth of her mind, she hoped for the Promised One. It was not to be. The child first born to the first couple was, as the scripture notes, fathered by Adam. He was not the Seed of the woman conceived by the Holy Spirit, as the Christ would be. The child's name was Cain. Eve gave birth again. The child's name was Abel. The children inherited their father's nature. (Gen. 4:1–2)

Years passed, more children were born, and, on a certain day, Cain and Abel made offerings to the Lord. Picture a public gathering. Cain is officiating. Cain, as the first born, has the honor and prestige as the leader in worship. He offers a meal offering. The scriptures call it a "meat offering." Leviticus chapter 2 describes it: fine flour unleavened, with oil and incense and burned before the Lord. Not at all was the offering a few vegetables offered by a well-meaning but ignorant savage.

Now, picture Cain offering, from his own efforts, a sacrifice without bloodshed, without death, as a sin penalty to represent the coming Deliverer. Nevertheless, to the public, no doubt, it was a beautiful offering, sweet smelling to man and one produced by Cain from his hard work on the land.

But the Lord has no respect for it. The Hebrew scriptures indicate the Lord turns His face from it, as if it smells bad (Gen. 4:5).

Now, Abel, the younger brother, makes offerings. He, too, makes a meat offering, as the scripture makes plain, but also a sin offering. "And Abel, he also brought of the firstlings of his flock and the fat thereof" (Gen. 4:4). The Lord honors Abel's offerings, with respect.

What humiliation to Cain! Cain is furious. The Lord tells him that if he had done well, he would have been accepted. There were problems with Cain's offering. First, he didn't offer well because his life didn't fit the statement his offering proclaimed. The fine flour, unleavened, in the meat offering, represents a pure life without the evil leaven represents.

Furthermore, the oil represents the Holy Spirit blessing and giving power to the life. The incense represents a life dedicated to prayer and godliness. Cain didn't fit these qualities. He didn't offer well. Had Cain lived a sinless life, he would have been accepted, and his offering would have been accepted. Cain needed to make a sin offering. A sacrifice in the manner that the Lord made for his parents when He clothed their nakedness. The sin offering, and any offering for atonement, was death by a substitute for the offerer who deserved death. The penalty transferred to the sacrifice, and the offerer freed from the penalty.

This is important for us to know and believe: the true offering and sacrifice was the Lord Jesus Christ. He is the true meat offering: the sinless life, anointed by the Holy Spirit, with life eternal, now at the right hand of God and on earth. His, a life of prayer and godliness. He also is the true sin offering. He, as the scriptures tell us, was made sin, who knew no sin, "that we might be made the righteousness of God in him."

The Lord had respect for Abel's offering because in it was the truth. He came as a sinner with faith in the Savior.

Yet, in the prophetic fulfillment of the offering of Abel we now have something better. For, since Jesus offered up His blood and was raised from the dead, we have, when we trust Him, our hearts sprinkled with His blood by the Holy Spirit and our conscience cleansed (Heb. 12:24).

The blood of Abel's sacrifice waxed old and decayed. It had to be repeated. Jesus the Christ had life in Himself. Not a drop of His blood has decayed. It is still covering the sin of the world and the heart of every believer's conscience. His sacrifice was "once for all" (Heb. 10:10). In the time of the Old Testament, God's people worshipped with offerings and sacrifices. Many of their sacrifices were beasts considered clean, such as sheep, cattle, or goats, whose flesh, on occasion, after the sacrifice, could be eaten after shedding its blood. Such sacrifices go back to the first one when the Lord clothed Adam and Eve with skins. The law of offering sacrifices was codified in the book of Leviticus, but the sacrificial theme runs through the entire Bible, for "without shedding of blood there is no remission of sin" (Heb. 9:22).

The Jewish sacrificial system ended in Jerusalem AD 70, when Titus, son of the Roman emperor Vespasian, commanding four legions, destroyed Jerusalem. The sacrifices were but a foretelling by illustration, fulfilled in the sacrifice of Christ, His holy life, death for our sins and, resurrection for our righteousness and acceptance by God. And, most interestingly, an illustration and teaching device for Christians in their worship of God with sacrificial offerings of themselves, a living sacrifice. "I beseech you therefore, brethren, by the mercies of God, that ye present your bodies a living sacrifice, holy, acceptable unto God, which is your reasonable service" (Rom. 12:1). (We will discuss this later, when we cross the Jordan River with the Hebrews.)

This is the Christian's true worship. Christ speaks of this worship. "Then said Jesus unto his disciples, If any man will come after me, let him deny himself, and take up the cross and follow me" (Matt. 16:24). The sacrifice here is a bloodless one, but we need to remember this: it is the blood of Jesus that saves us, not our own. In the book of Leviticus, the blood sacrifices of clean animals, a foreshadow of Christ's giving His blood on the cross, always preceded the bloodless sacrifice. Paul's urging to "present your bodies a living sacrifice" was written to Christians who already had faith (Romans 1:7–8).

It is as futile for a person to think he or she, as an unbeliever, can be accepted by good works as it was for Cain to make his bloodless meat offering. First must come repentance and faith in Jesus Christ, who died for our sins and was raised from the dead for our righteousness and justification. It is not by works of righteousness we have done, but by His mercy that we are accepted by God.

To illustrate: Douglas Corrigan became famous, in1938, for flying across the Atlantic in a single-engine plane he had constructed, but his adventure was a flight without approval. He flew from New York to Ireland, when his approved flight plan was to fly from New York to Long Beach, California. He claimed the change was result of heavy cloud cover that obscured landmarks. His trip took skill and courage, but, instead of approval, it drew censure. He is known as "Wrong Way Corrigan."

First faith, then works of faith, in going on the road to heaven: that is the right way on the right road. Good works don't put us on the road to heaven. They are the wrong way on the right road, no matter how noteworthy they might be.

One could hardly find a better demonstration of these statements than in the experience and testimony of John Wesley. Wesley, one of the chief founders of the Methodist movement within the Church of England, took passage to America, in 1735, as a missionary to the colony of Georgia. He was a graduate of Oxford, a keen scholar, and an ordained Anglican priest.

No one could have worked in America with more diligence than John Wesley in the "giving of life to the Lord." He preached daily in the language of the colonists, visited the sick, buried the dead, and led in weekly worship services in a mosquito- and disease-laden colony; however, his ministry was a failure.

Returning to England in 1738, a moral and professional failure, he wrote in his journal:

> It is now two years and four months since I left my native country in order to teach the Georgia Indians the nature of Christianity. But what have I found myself in the meantime? Why, (what I least of all expected), that I, who went to America to convert others was never myself converted to God.[4]

The Lord was merciful to Wesley. He called him by the testimony of his brother, Charles, and an exposition by Martin

---

[4] John Wesley, *Works of John Wesley, Journal 1* (Grand Rapids, MI: Baker Publishing Group, a reprint from the 1872 edition issued by Wesleyan Methodist Bookroom, London, England), 75–76.

Luther on salvation by faith alone. Wesley writes of the final event in 1738, on May 24:

> In the evening, I went, very unwillingly, to a society in Aldersgate street where one was reading Luther's preface to the Epistle to the Romans. About a quarter before nine, while he was describing the change which God works in the heart through faith in Christ, I felt my heart strangely warmed. I felt I did trust in Christ, Christ alone for salvation. And an assurance was given to me, that He had taken away my sins, even mine, and saved me from the law of sin and death."[5]

But let us not forget that Jesus said, "suffer the little children to come unto me and forbid them not for of such is the Kingdom of God." Doubtless there are many children, who, living in a Christian home, have heard and believed the gospel. Looking to the living Christ, they have asked Him to come into their hearts. So, believing He died for their sins, they are saved. Later on, in giving their lives to Christ, they fulfill Romans 12:1, an act of approved worship, a living sacrifice, which God blesses. So, they really do give their lives to Christ, and He accepts their worship. (We will visit this subject again when we go "Into the Land of Giants.")

On the other hand, to make one's own religious works, even the extremes of martyrdom and self-denial, the grounds for acceptance by God is the "way of Cain," a wrong way on the right road.

---

[5] John Wesley, *Works of John Wesley, Journal 1*, 103.

The Lord expects us to make our calling and election sure (2 Pet. 1:8). It is " … fruitful in the knowledge of our Lord Jesus Christ," not a looking on old works and depending on them. They are a rotten foundation and crumble in temptation. Rather, we must look on Christ, seeing Him who is invincible, as in 1 Corinthians 15:2, "saved if you keep in memory." What God does shall "be forever"; true faith, the gift of God, continues. So, Paul could say, "I have kept the faith." We must continue on, in the belief that "Christ died for our sins according to Scripture and on the third day rose again according to the Scriptures." Here is the election of grace coupled with human responsibility. Both are in the hands of God. "Who shall lay anything to the charge of God's elect? It is God that justifieth" (Rom. 8:33).

Sadly, many Bible teachers and commentators of Christendom would place us under law's righteousness to establish our own righteousness, ignoring or forgetting the righteousness of Christ credited (imputed) to all who believe. Result: ignoring or forgetting the righteousness of Christ, which the Holy Spirit places in the heart of each person who believes. And so, the way of Cain continues and prospers in blindness against repeated directions in scripture. "Not by works of righteousness which we have done but according to his mercy he saved us, by the washing of regeneration, and renewing of the Holy Ghost" (Titus 3:5).

CHAPTER 5

❧❀❧

THE WAY THROUGH THE FLOOD

In the tenth generation from the first man, Adam, one named Lamech called his newborn son Noah, which means "rest." Lamech said, "This same shall comfort us concerning our work" (Gen. 5:29).

From one standpoint, Noah had little time for rest in his labor in his lifetime, but he rested on the promises of God. He lived when, as is nearly so today, "the wickedness of man was great in the earth and that every imagination of the thoughts of his heart was only evil continually" (Gen. 6:5). Considering this, the Lord said, "I will destroy man whom I have created from the face of the earth; both man and beast, and the creeping things and the fowls of the air; for it repenteth me that I have made them" (Gen. 6:7). It was otherwise for Noah. He was a just man and walked with God, for he had found grace in the eyes of the Lord. Then came the great flood. It brought death, leaving only Noah and his family alive from among all the descendants of Adam. They found safety in a huge ark Noah had built at the specifications given to him by the Lord. We shall see how the ark's deliverance is an object lesson of the path to our own safety in the judgment of sin, which is coming on ungodly mankind: "it is appointed unto men once to die, but after this the judgment" (Heb. 9:27).

It was the worst of times. Bloody crimes, rape, war, broken treaties, sexual deviations all were the order of the day. It didn't need to be so. The testimony of Adam, the example of Abel, the warning of Cain, and the promise of the coming Messiah were fresh in memory. Moreover, a mighty preacher, a man who walked with God, named Enoch, of the seventh generation from Adam, blazed his warning to generation after generation. He preached righteousness and the judgment to come (Jude 14). Then, a mighty miracle took place. God took Enoch to heaven without Enoch dying. "He was not for God took him." He simply disappeared before their eyes. Was there a turning to God? There was not. The Spirit of God had strived with mankind—to no avail. God then warned that if there was no repentance, mankind would be cut off—put down and destroyed—and His Spirit would cease; His work on mankind's conscience would be over. Still, their hearts hardened in rebellion and wickedness.

And here is a foreshadower of our sin and Christ's eternal salvation:

> The longsuffering of God waited in the days of Noah, while the ark was preparing, wherein few, that is, eight souls were saved by water. The like figure whereunto even baptism doth also now save us (not the putting away of the filth of the flesh, but the answer of a good conscience toward God) by the resurrection of Jesus Christ; Who is gone into heaven and is on the right hand of God: angels and authorities and powers being made subject to him. (1 Pet. 3:20–22)

The grace of the Lord Jesus, the Son of God, comes on the scene before judgment by the great flood. A sinner named Noah finds God's grace (undeserved mercy) (Gen. 6:8). After Noah finds grace, we read that he "was a just man and perfect in his generations." God thereupon provides safety for Noah and his family. No men in God's sight are just without first being changed by the grace of God and righteousness imputed. In this instance, as to mankind, "every imagination of his heart was only evil continually." That included Noah because "not by works of righteousness which we have done but by His mercy he saves us."

Good works that count follow but never precede faith:

> But God, who is rich in mercy, for his great love wherewith he loved us, Even when we were dead in sins, hath quickened us together with Christ, (by grace ye are saved;), And hath raised us up together, and made us sit together in heavenly places in Christ Jesus: That in the ages to come he might shew the exceeding riches of his grace in his kindness toward us through Christ Jesus. For by grace are ye saved

> through faith; and that not of yourselves: it is the gift
> of God: Not of works, lest any man should boast.
> For we are his workmanship, created in Christ Jesus
> unto good works, which God hath before ordained
> that we should walk in them. (Eph. 2:4–10)

God told Noah, years in advance, that destruction was coming with the "end of all flesh"—judgment because of the violence on earth. He advises Noah to build an ark (a large ship), and gives Noah the specifics for the building. We will note this: at the beginning of the specifics, God says, "pitch it within and without with pitch." An astonishing fact: The Old Testament of the Bible, in this portion, was written in Hebrew, and the word for *pitch,* in Hebrew, is the same as the word for *atonement.* This is true throughout the Old Testament. Think of the implications. The idea is for a protective covering. "And Aaron shall bring the bullock of the sin-offering, which is for himself, and shall make an atonement for himself, and for his house, and shall kill the bullock of the sin-offering which is for himself" (Lev. 16:11).

The sacrifices of the Old Testament were but pictures and reminders of the true atonement (covering): the Christ whose blood is our atonement. It was in the ark alone that Noah and his family found safety and rode out the flood. That which made the ark waterproof was the pitch within and without. That which secures our safety from the judgment to come is the atonement of Christ, and nothing else. Our protection is His blood shed on the cross of Calvary:

> For all have sinned, and come short of the glory of
> God; Being justified freely by his grace through the
> redemption that is in Christ Jesus: Whom God hath
> set forth to be a propitiation through faith in his
> blood, to declare his righteousness for the remission
> of sins that are past, through the forbearance of
> God. (Rom. 3:23–25)

Notice, too, that the pitch was within and without the ark's structure. It was visible to God from above and to Noah within the ark; a surety of safety from the floodwater. So, too, does the blood of Christ give us assurance of Christ's death, His being a substitute for us and from our sins. From above, God sees His law justified in Christ's sinless life yielded up on our behalf, and us in Christ by faith. Not only was Christ a man; he was truly man and God. "Who shall lay a charge against God's elect? It is God that justifies." The Creator and Judge of the universe has taken our place on the sentencing dock of justice, in place of our shortcomings and for our breaking His law.

God gave the specifics to Noah. Noah then builds the ark according to God's specifications. In other words, Noah built by faith in God's word (Heb. 11:7). You may ask, "What work would God have me do?"

The scripture gives the answer. "Then said they unto him, What shall we do that we might work the works of God? Jesus answered and said unto them, This is the work of God, that ye believe on him whom he hath sent" (John 6:28–29). Believe in Christ, and keep on believing. Here is the mystery of living the Christian life in this wicked world, in a body that still has the flesh contending in it. We "walk by faith." Many, I am afraid, make a great mistake here. Believing they are born again by faith, which they are, they think it is then up to them to keep their salvation by their own efforts. The words of the old song come to mind: "The arm of flesh will fail you, ye dare not trust your own." In the journey to God's heavenly city, we would do well to keep Paul's testimony in mind:

> I am crucified with Christ: nevertheless I live: yet not I, but Christ liveth in me: and the life which I now live in the flesh I live by the faith of the Son of God, who loved me, and gave himself for me. I do not frustrate the grace of God: for if righteousness come by the law, then Christ is dead in vain. (Gal. 2:20–21)

Well-meaning but uninformed zealots and monks have tortured the flesh to no avail to get mastery over it. They have gone to the extreme of starving themselves, castrating themselves, and such, forgetting—if they ever knew—that if the Son (Jesus) shall make you free, you shall be free indeed:

> "Jesus answered them, 'Verily, verily, I say unto you, Whosoever committeth sin is the servant of sin. And the servant abideth not in the house forever: but the Son abideth ever. If the Son therefore shall make you free, ye shall be free indeed.'" (John 8:34–36)

I have found that, whatever the temptation, if one by faith turns it, in all its unvarnished reality, over to the Spirit that resides within, the temptation will disappear. Jesus has promised to never leave or forsake the believer. By His Spirit, He is ever within the believer. He does not cheat. He does not steal. He does not blame God. He does not lie. He does not lust. He does not harbor a grudge. He loves and forgives. He is present and "greater is he that is in you than he that is in the world" (1 John 4:4). So, then, as we walk by faith and "work out our salvation," the ark of salvation is ever present. We begin the journey by faith alone, and we keep on the journey by faith alone. This is the victory that overcomes the world.

Noah not only built by God's instructions but by God's instructions alone. By eagerness to avoid the destruction God had declared coming, he could have run on ahead, gotten his own plans mixed with God's, and built the ark in a way than he otherwise did. Had he done so, he would have endangered his life and the lives of his family. God knows what is coming and what we need. We don't. Let us build by faith in God's word alone. In many ways, the history of religion shows an eagerness and lack of faith, with many presumptions, much like a boy sitting on the bench during a ball game, shouting to the coach, "Send me in, send me in." And when the coach does send him in, the outcome is damage to the team and not the heroics of the boy's imagination. Adding to God's directions has, as the history of religion shows, disastrous results. The ship that Noah built was covered with pitch. It was not pretty. It was not a pleasure cruiser. Its journey was rough.

To illustrate: as a result of the nation of Israel's disobedience many years later, after the law was given, they lost the famed ark of the covenant. This ark was a small box to be in the Holy of Holies room of the tabernacle (tent of worship). It carried the Ten Commandments engraved in stone, brought down from Mount Sinai by Moses. Over it was the gold mercy seat where the blood of the sin offering was sprinkled once each year, between two gold cherubim. Over the mercy seat of gold was the literal presence of God, a cloud by day and a fire by night, to lead and protect the chosen nation. Israel sinned and kept on disobeying God. Consequently, they lost the ark in battle. Years of suffering came.

Then, David came to the throne as king: Israel turned back to God. David found where the ark, the centerpiece showing the nation's faith, was located. He directed its return to Israel. Here is the record:

> And they set the ark of God upon a new cart, and brought it out of the house of Abinadab that was in Gibeah: and Uzzah and Ahio, the sons of Abinadab, drove the new cart. And they brought it out of the house of Abinadab which was at Bibeah, accompanying the ark of God: and Ahio went before the ark. And David and all the house of Israel played before the Lord on all manner of instruments made of fir wood, even on harps, and on psalteries, and on timbrels, and on cornets, and on cymbals. And when they came to Nachon's threshing floor, Uzzah put forth his hand to the ark of God, and took hold of it; for the oxen shook it. And the anger of the Lord was kindled against Uzzah; and God smote him there for his error; and there he died by the ark of God. (2 Sam. 6:3–7)

This man Uzzah died, not trusting but wanting to prop God up. Can we learn the lesson? "Not with wisdom of words, lest the cross of Christ should be made of none effect" (1 Cor. 1:17). God's work does not need to be propped up by parties, worldly showmanship, and schemes. He is able to provide.

There is and always has been only one way to God, as Jesus tells us: "no man cometh unto the Father, but by me" (John 14:6).

Noah's ark, a great ship, by foreshadow, teaches us this same important truth. The ark had one door for entrance, and only one. Moreover, it had one window above, and only one. Christ is the door. Our eye fixed above, where Christ is on the right hand of the Majesty on high, is our assurance in time of storm.

The great ship built before their eyes was finished after years of God's forbearance and warning. Yet there was no repentance among men. Noah remains faithful. It is the time of God's judgment. He calls Noah, his family, and the animals, by numbers specified, in the ark. They enter. Noah comes in last. Fearsome words appear in scripture: "and the Lord shut him in." When the Lord shuts the door, no one can open it. He, and He alone, has the keys of death. We get a picture of the Lord Jesus after His resurrection as He appeared to His messenger and friend, John:

> And when I saw him, I fell at his feet as dead. And he laid his right hand upon me, saying unto me, "Fear not: I am the first and the last. I am he that liveth, and was dead; and, behold, I am alive for

evermore, Amen; and have the keys of hell and of death." (Rev. 1:17–18)

For the multitude of people outside the ark, it was too late. God, in His mercy, had extended Noah's time for 120 years after warning. The day of grace was over. Here is the record:

> And the flood was forty days upon the earth; and the waters increased, and bare up the ark, and it was lift up above the earth. And the waters prevailed, and were increased greatly upon the earth; and the ark went upon the face of the waters. And the waters prevailed exceedingly upon the earth; and all the high hills, that were under the whole heaven, were covered. Fifteen cubits upward did the waters prevail; and the mountains were covered. And all flesh died that moved upon the earth, both of fowl, and of cattle, and of beast, and of every creeping thing that creepeth upon the earth and every man: All in whose nostrils was the breath of life, of all that was in the dry land, died. And every living substance was destroyed which was upon the face of the ground, both man, and cattle, and the creeping things, and the fowl of the heaven; and they were destroyed from the earth: and Noah only remained alive, and they that were with him in the ark. And the waters prevailed upon the earth an hundred and fifty days. (Gen. 7:17–24)

There never had been, since the world began, such a rainstorm, and there will never be such again. Picture it: darkness, the earth opening with waterspouts, the heavens collapsing, no escape, little rafts losing their way, bodies floating, swimmers giving up.

It was being in the ark built to God's specifications that saved Noah from the storm. Nothing else. The religious could pray. The rich could flee in their chariots to higher ground, and no safety came.

The neighbors of Noah could knock on the door of the ark. No relief, because God had shut the door. In all the storm, the ones in the ark were safe. No one else. All others perished.

The ark took the blows of the raging storm. So, Christ crucified took on the cross the blows of God's judgment on sin. It was no little thing when God's Son bore our sins "in his own body" on the cross, as the scripture says, in 1 Peter 2:24. Here, in striking prophecy, are the words of the One who became sin for all who believe, taking our sins on Himself:

> Then said I, "Lo, I come: in the volume of the book it is written of me. I delight to do thy will, O my God: yea, thy law is within my heart." I have preached righteousness in the great congregation: lo, I have not refrained my lips, O Lord, thou knowest. I had not hid thy righteousness within my heart; I have declared thy faithfulness and thy salvation: I have not concealed thy loving kindness and thy truth from the great congregation. Withhold not thou thy tender mercies from me, O Lord: let thy loving kindness and thy truth continually preserve me. For innumerable evils have compassed me about: mine iniquities have taken hold upon me, so that I am not able to look up; they are more than the hairs of mine head: therefore my heart faileth me. Be pleased, O Lord, to deliver me: O Lord make haste to help me. (Ps. 40:7–13)

Here, we find what Christ experienced, being made sin, all kinds of sin, dying for our sins.

And He did it to do the will of His heavenly Father, who would be just and yet justify the ungodly. God accepted this sacrifice, raising Jesus, His Christ, from the dead, where he now reigns, giving us who believe His righteousness.

Let Noah and his safety in the flood remind us: When life's storm does come, then, in Christ, we are safe. And that day— when we stand before the eternal Judge—we are safe in Christ. Our works will be judged, but our sins are already judged, since Christ, for our sins, once and for all died on the cross, taking our sentence on Himself. Rewards will be ours, for our works of faith—just as, after the flood, the Lord brought Noah and his family to dry ground, blessing them with a renewed earth, safety, and prosperity (Gen. 8:16–9:17). Our Lord Jesus said, "And whosoever shall give to drink unto one of these little ones a cup of cold water only in the name of a disciple, verily I say unto you, he shall in no wise lose his reward" (Matt. 10:42).

CHAPTER 6

THE TWO ROADS

Thankfully, there are lighted signposts along the road to God's eternal city. When we are on a new highway, the question comes to us: Am I still on the right road? The sign that provides the highway number we want gives us assurance. The road to the heavenly city goes through enemy territory. There are dangers. It is a new way we have not gone before. It is a way of faith. "Faith comes by hearing and hearing by the word of God," so let us hear and understand God's Word in our heart and mind, lest we be overcome by doubt or discouragement and, consequently, turn aside.

One of the signposts designating the way and illuminating it is the call to, conversion of, and sons born to father Abraham, first called Abram. God's signposts do more than just repeat. They give light and explanation that encourage us and build up our faith while simultaneously illuminating the way. God called

Abram in a city of spiritual darkness, where people worshipped the moon. This was little more than two hundred years after the idolatry preceding the flood prevailed. It is remarkable how quickly mankind fails. Here is the record:

> Now the Lord had said unto Abram, "Get thee out of thy country, and from thy kindred, and from thy father's house, unto a land that I will shew thee: And I will make of thee a great nation, and I will bless thee, and make thy name great; and thou shalt be a blessing: And I will bless them that bless thee, and curse him that curseth thee: and in thee shall all families of the earth be blessed." (Gen. 12:1–3)

Abram responded by faith; that is, he believed God. He began his journey, looking for a city whose builder and maker was God. He left his home, going out on a new way into a new land, walking by faith alone. He took with him his wife and his property and kin, but no map and no guide other than the Spirit of God. That is enough. God blessed him with prosperity and safety, the respect of his friends and enemies, and, in fact, everything but a son for an heir. But this exception was to change. And herein is one of the great events marking spiritual truth and world history to this day. In the events of Abram's sons, we have an allegory of the two roads to God's heavenly city. One of the roads is the road of faith. The other is a road of law and works, and it is a dead end.

Here is how it began:

> And Abram said, "Lord God, what wilt thou give me, seeing I go childless, and the steward of my

house is this Eliezer of Damascus?" And Abram said, "Behold, to me thou has given me no seed: and, lo, one born in my house is mine heir." (Gen. 15:2–3)

There was a problem for Abram. His wife, Sarai, had no children and was elderly, but she had a personal slave named Hagar, an Egyptian. It was a social disgrace in those days for a woman to be childless, but custom had provided a remedy. The childless woman could designate a surrogate, give the surrogate to her husband to mate, and then a child born from this union was considered the child of the childless wife. This is what Sarai did:

> And Sarai said unto Abram, "Behold now, the Lord hath restrained me from bearing: I pray thee, go in unto my maid; it may be that I may obtain children by her." And Abram hearkened to the voice of Sarai. (Gen. 16:2)

A child was born from the union of Abram and Hagar. His name was Ishmael. Hagar was a proud woman. Instead of accepting her lot as Sarai's servant, she did the contrary. She began lording it over Sarai that she, Hagar, had borne a son to Abram. She despised Sarai, her mistress and owner.

Sarai dealt strongly in the matter. She put Hagar down, reminding her that she was a slave and Ishmael belonged to Sarai. Hagar, proud woman that she was, couldn't tolerate this treatment. She ran off into the desert wilderness without supply.

The Lord God rescued Hagar where she was camping by an oasis and sent her back to Sarai, telling her to submit herself to Sarai. Hagar gave outward obedience but raised the child Ishmael with resentment, as later conflict shows. Still, Abram wanted the Lord to accept and honor Ishmael. Abram, ninety-nine years old, was waiting when the Lord God appeared to him again. The Lord changed his name from Abram (high father) to Abraham (father of nations). The Lord changed Sarai's name to Sarah (princess) and promised a son to be born to this aged couple. This son was to be the ancestor of the Seed (Christ), and a covenant through this Seed was to be everlasting. Abraham laughed when he heard God's promise, because Sarah was ninety years old and he would soon be one hundred.

Sarah laughed too when the Lord told her she would give birth to a son. The son was born (as the Lord promised), and he was named Isaac (laughter).

Hagar, the Egyptian servant, once again entered the picture. Her son, the servant boy Ishmael, now about fourteen years of age, saw the baby boy Isaac, his half brother, being weaned, and mocked him. Did Ishmael do a pantomime of a helpless baby waving his arms about, sucking and crying? Likely. Hagar was only a slave. Sarah was furious:

> And Sarah saw the son of Hagar the Egyptian, which she had born unto Abraham, mocking. Wherefore, she said unto Abraham, "Cast out this bondwoman and her son: for the son of this bondwoman shall not be heir with my son, even with Isaac. (Gen. 21:9–10)

The Lord God directed Abraham to do as Sarah had ordered, but promised to bless and make a nation of the descendants of Ishmael.

Abraham personally gave Hagar bread and water, and sent her off. Hagar, in a huff no doubt, proud as she was, went into the wilderness, along with Ishmael, and no supplies. She could have taken a caravan of supplies. Abraham was very wealthy. He was a king, stronger and more powerful than his neighboring tribes and kingdoms. He loved Ishmael, but he could not deal with the haughty Hagar—nor could Sarah.

Hagar found herself in the desert, water gone, food gone, and Ishmael about to die of thirst. The Lord God rescued her, showing nearby water. She and, later, Ishmael (his wife an Egyptian) prospered. No doubt at Abraham's expense (Gen. 21:13–21).

This account of Sarah and Hagar is one that the scripture later calls an allegory. The points it raises are of vital importance. When first called an allegory, churches in Galatia were about to leave the doctrine of salvation by faith alone in God's grace and mix it with the law, thereby losing their place and going into apostasy:

> Tell me, ye that desire to be under the law, do ye not hear the law? For it is written, that Abraham had two sons, the one by a bondmaid, the other by a freewoman. But he who was of the bondwoman was born after the flesh; but he of the freewoman was by promise. Which things are an allegory: for these are

> the two covenants; the one from the mount Sinai,
> which gendereth to bondage, which is Agar. For
> this Agar is mount Sinai in Arabia, and answereth
> to Jerusalem which now is, and is in bondage with
> her children. But Jerusalem which is above is free,
> which is the mother of us all. (Gal. 4:21–26)

Here are, at least, some of the comparisons in the allegory of Hagar-Ishmael and Sarai-Isaac. Hagar came out of Egypt. So, too, was the law added on Mount Sinai as the nation Israel came out of Egypt. It was added "because of transgressions." In short, God gave it to show His people what sin is. Israel, living in Egypt as slaves, had taken on the gross sins of their neighbors. This is very evident in their building a golden calf idol, which they then worshipped, their bodies naked in a sexual debauch, immediately upon receiving the law from Moses after he descended Mount Sinai. Does the law—the Ten Commandments—have relevance today? Of course. Listen to the apostle Paul, the Lord's special messenger:

> Desiring to be teachers of the law; understanding
> neither what they say, nor whereof they affirm.
> But we know that the law is good, if a man use it
> lawfully; Knowing this, that the law is not made for
> a righteous man, but for the lawless and disobedient,
> for the ungodly and for sinners, for unholy and
> profane, for murderers of fathers and murderers
> of mothers, for manslayers, For whoremongers,
> for them that defile themselves with mankind, for
> menstealers, for liars, for perjured persons, and if
> there be any other thing that is contrary to sound
> doctrine; According to the glorious gospel of the

blessed God, which was committed to my trust. (1 Tim. 1:7–11)

And the lovely Hagar is kept alive today in the law she represents; however, she is not the promise of Christ to come. Neither is she the power of the believer to walk the Christlike way, nor does she represent the forgiveness of sins. The law she represents shows the need for the promise of grace.

Could we not say that in this country, in colonial times, Jonathan Edwards was a gifted law preacher, and his complement, George Whitfield, a gifted grace preacher? And, later, was not Charles Finney a gifted law preacher? Surely, we can agree that D. L. Moody was a gifted grace preacher. They did not mix the two. And yet, with all these blessings and more preachers of the truth in modern times, this nation has drifted farther and farther away from our Lord. Consider this tragic warning from God's Word to all of us who are traveling on the way, and to our neighbors: "The wicked shall be turned into hell and all the nations that forget God" (Ps. 9:17).

Abraham and Sarah turned to the young Hagar, in their own physical weakness and, frankly, in weak dependence on God. They were old. Sarah was past the age when a woman could conceive a child. The Lord had promised them a child. They wanted to have that promise fulfilled in the worst way; the marvelous promise of the forerunner and ancestor of the Seed, the Messiah. So, in their weakness, they turned to Hagar. Abraham united with Hagar. She conceived and bore Ishmael.

The above picture reflects and foreshadows the weakness of young believers in Christ, who, in their weakness to overcome sin in their lives, turn in self-reliance, looking to God's law for their strength and fulfillment. Paul speaks of this experience in the seventh chapter of Romans:

> I find then a law, that, when I would do good, evil is present with me. For I delight in the law of God after the inward man: But I see another law in my members, warring against the law of my mind, and bringing me into captivity to the law of sin which is in my members. O wretched man that I am! Who shall deliver me from the body of this death? (Rom. 7:21–24)

We can't stay there. The answer comes in the next chapter of Romans:

> For the law of the Spirit of life in Christ Jesus hath made me free from the law of sin and death. For what law could not do, in that it was weak through the flesh, God sending his own Son in the likeness of sinful flesh, and for sin, condemned sin in the flesh: That the righteousness of the law might be fulfilled in us, who walk not after the flesh, but after the Spirit. (Rom. 8:2–4)

So, Sarah said, "Cast out the bondwoman (Hagar) and her son (Ishmael)." We must, walking in the way, do the same; that is, walk in the power of the Holy Spirit, turning temptation over to Him who resides within, since we were born again from above by faith. He has said, "I will never leave you nor forsake you." (More on this subject later; so important it is.)

A law-bound Christian is like a prisoner freed from prison who will not accept freedom and who continues in prison under the law of sin and death. Such a person is like a root-bound plant. The roots grow inward, the old, dead fiber, and fail to reach out for nourishment.

We who believe in Christ can turn our particular bondage—whether a habit or whatever it might be—over to the Deliverer, the Spirit of Christ within. Then, the doors of the prison open. The jailer is gone. Freedom comes (Rom. 8:2).

Another push to the wrong road can come from one's concern over a lack of personal holiness. Satan's accusations here would, if we permit, turn one back to leaning on the law; this, in an attempt to do right! (2 Cor. 11:14).

May the Lord help us to remember to confess our shortcomings and yield ourselves to Him: "He is faithful and just to forgive." It is His Spirit that gives power to walk in good conscience. The law is good, but we, by nature, are not. Walking and depending on one's commitment to works or law puts one on a dead-end street to failure. (I not only refer to the law of Moses but also include those works of law written on the conscience of Jew and Gentile alike—law as a principle [Rom. 2].)

A story from a frustrating cattle drive illustrates this. On a hot summer day, a rider on horseback is moving one hundred or so cattle to water in the sand hills of Nebraska. The watering tank that had watered the herd now has nothing but mud in it. The water pump on the windmill is broken. In the adjoining pasture runs the Calamus River, with plenty of clean water. Its pasture has been secured by a fence and gate, so the rider goes on ahead and opens the gate. He begins to move the thirsty cattle on the trail to the river pasture. He rides a good horse; and with him is a good dog, a collie, at least as much use in a brief cattle drive as two more mounted men. The drive starts on the three-mile trek, winding between the hills. The cattle follow a visible cow trail. About halfway, and before reaching the gate to the river pasture, the rider becomes alarmed. The herd strung out on the trail begin to trot along instead of going at their usual meandering pace. The rider knows that shortly before the gate, the trail forks: to the right, it goes to the open gate and the river; to the left, it goes around a little hill and then back to the tank with nothing in it but mud.

The rider thinks that he can move the herd to the right trail at the fork, but he doesn't expect what has happened. The wind, blowing hard, has caught up the scent of the moisture in the tank of mud. The herd leaders smell it and turn back, going on the left fork of the trail. The rider and his dog race to the front of the herd. It is too late. The cattle break into a headlong rush and stampede.

Fearing the exhaustion and perhaps death of the herd, the rider, with his dog, goes back to the tank of mud where the herd is gathering. He starts the drive anew. Darkness comes; but the herd must reach the river. Another day in the burning sun may mean death for many.

So it is for any who, becoming discouraged, turn from the walk of faith to go back under law. The water of life is not there. The water of life is in the word and life of Christ, made present to us by His Holy Spirit. Peter, Christ's special messenger, made a good example when many of Christ's disciples turned from following Him to go back into Judaism. "Then said Jesus unto the twelve, Will ye also go away? Then Simon Peter answered him, Lord to whom shall we go? thou hast the words of eternal life" (John 6:67–68).

God promised Abraham a son borne by Sarah, his wife, for an everlasting covenant and with his seed after him. As for Ishmael, He promised blessings on his descendants to be a great nation.

After Isaac was born, Abraham never faltered. Rather, he rested in God's promise: a good example. There remains a "rest for the children of God."

It may appear that spiritual growth is slow in a new convert to Christ, but growth it is, not dead works. To put oneself under the law and to hurry up the process of mature Christian living I compare to moving down to a street the neighbors called Do-Better Street. Of course, that wasn't the official name, but that is what it was called in a joking manner. The houses on Do-Better Street were not up to par in comparison to the rest of the neighborhood. It was said that the people who lived there commented, "We are just here until we can do better." And they lived on Do-Better Street for the rest of their lives. Lesson: Cease from living in and looking to works; instead, accept the beautiful finished work of Christ, and rest in it, looking to His Spirit. When the sap comes up the tree, last year's dead leaves fall off the limbs; and if they don't, the Forester (our Lord) knows what to do. (For more on this in scripture, refer to Colossians 3:5–10.)

Ishmael mocked Isaac when he was being weaned. Just so, legalists belittle young believers for not living up to their high standards; yet they themselves don't live up to those standards, and they feel quite superior in their exalted position. It was the same in biblical times:

> And after these things he went forth, and saw a publican, named Levi, sitting at the receipt of custom: and he said unto him, "Follow me." And he left all, rose up, and followed him. And Levi made him a great feast in his own house: and there was a great company of publicans and of others that sat down with them. But their scribes and Pharisees murmured against his disciples, saying, "Why do ye eat and drink with publicans and sinners?" (Luke 5:27–30)

Consider this situation. Two men have a debt, each one on a note of a million dollars. They are not eligible for bankruptcy. They are about to lose their homes and their all to the creditors. Along comes a benefactor. He deposits a million dollars in each debtor's bank account. One debtor gladly uses it to pay off his million-dollar note. The other debtor claims to be one "who pays his own debts" and refuses the gift. "I will pay it myself, for I am a responsible person," he says. Fact is, he can't even pay the interest, so the debt keeps increasing. Question: Which debtor honors his note? Obviously, the one who accepted the gift.

And so, too, do we who take Christ's payment in full for debt to the law for our sins honor the law. Those who look to themselves do not. And for them and their willful refusal of God's grace, as the scripture says, "he that is unjust, let him be unjust still" (Rev. 22:11). Their dishonor to the law keeps increasing, forever, unless they repent.

And that isn't all. When born again by faith in Christ Jesus, God, by a miracle, gives us a new nature, the predominant characteristic of which is love—the kind of love that seeks the best for our fellow man. "Love fulfills the law." "But as many as received him, to them gave the power to become the sons of God, even to them that believe on his name: Which were born, not of blood, nor of the will of the flesh, nor of the will of man, but of God" (John 1:12–13). This is God's love. "And we have known and believed the love that God hath to us. God is love; and he that dwelleth in love dwelleth in God, and God in him" (1 John 4:16). Words fail to explain the greatness of God's love. This verse attempts:

> Could we with ink the ocean fill and were the skies of parchment made, were every stalk on earth a quill and every man a scribe by trade, to write the love of God above would drain the ocean dry. Nor could the scroll contain the whole though stretched from sky to sky.

One doesn't steal from another whom one loves. One doesn't seduce the spouse of another whom one loves. One doesn't hate or disregard the best interest of another whom he loves. Love fulfills the law.

The fruits of law and the fruits of grace are typified in the lives of Ishmael and Isaac. Ishmael was a wild man. His hand was against everyone. Isaac was a peaceable and tractable man. When others destroyed the wells he dug for his flocks, he moved on and dug a new well, forgiving instead of fighting, until, finally, he was left alone by his enemies.

A dangerous doctrine in Christendom is the mingling of law and grace. As Luther explained:

> It seemeth but a light matter to mingle the law and the gospel, faith and works together; but it doth more harm than a man's reason can conceive, for it taketh away Christ with all His benefits, and overthroweth the gospel, as Paul saith. The cause of this great evil is our flesh, which being plunged in sins, seeth no way how to get out, but by works, and therefore it would live in the righteousness of the law, and rest in the confidence of its own works.[6]

Can one envision the turmoil in Abraham's house had Sarah with Isaac and Hagar with Ishmael continued to live together? Never a quiet moment—constant fighting and constant accusations. To repeat a passage cited earlier: "And if by grace, then is it no more of works: otherwise grace is no more grace.

---

[6] Martin Luther, *Commentary on the Galatians*, 25.

74

But if it be of works, then is it no more grace: otherwise work is no more work" (Rom. 11:6).

One more way law and grace are mixed: the notion that Christ fulfilled the ceremonial law, but we believers are still under the moral law. That anyone would believe that doctrine is an amazement. It is refuted in reason and repeatedly in the Holy Scriptures.

The book of Galatians speaks of the law of circumcision (the act of entry to men who accept Judaism), which wrongly became an issue of the one obligation to young believers, with this quotation from the law itself: "Cursed be he that confirmeth not all the words of this law to do them" (Deut. 27:26). That is all the law of Moses. One cannot take the law apart, say, just keeping the seventh day, Sabbath, or just observing the Ten Commandments or some ceremony, as the sole requirement.

If we take one law for righteousness, we are under obligation to keep all the rest; otherwise, the scripture says we are cursed. "For whosoever shall keep the whole law and yet offend in one part, he is guilty of all" (James 2:10). Thanks be to God, though: "For Christ is the end of the law for righteousness to everyone that believeth" (Rom. 10:4).

The "ceremonial" law of the Old Testament, though rigorous in its demands, could be fully kept. The rich young ruler did it:

> And he said, "All these have I kept from my youth up." Now when Jesus heard these things, he said unto him, "Yet lackest thou one thing: sell all that

thou hast, and distribute unto the poor, and thou
shalt have treasure in heaven: and come, follow me."
(Luke 18:21–22)

The apostle Paul (if, indeed, the two were not the same person)
did it before his conversion. "What shall we say then? Is the
law sin? God forbid. Nay, I had not known sin, but by the law:
for I had not known lust, except the law had said, thou shalt
not covet" (Rom. 7:7). And Paul said of himself, "Touching the
righteousness which is in the law, blameless" (Phil. 3:6). The
moral law can be kept by no child of Adam. The ceremonial
law can be, and has been, kept.

Why did the eternal Son of God, Christ Jesus, take the burden
of our sins in His body, separated from His heavenly Father,
nailed naked to a wooden cross of His own free will, if only to
fulfill the ceremonial law? In other words, why did Christ die
if only for a ceremonial law that a person could keep naturally?

The Holy Scriptures plainly says to Gentile, non-Jewish believers
that the ordinances (laws) of God that were against them were
nailed to the cross. "Blotting out the handwriting of ordinances
that was against us, which was contrary to us, and took it out
of the way, nailing it to his cross" (Col. 2:14). The Colossians
were, for the most, part Gentiles. They were not, and never had
been, under the ceremonial law of the Old Testament. The law,
then, including the Ten Commandments, is nailed to Christ's
cross—but for believers only. All unbelievers are making a book
recording every act to be opened and judged under God"s law
(Rom.2:15-16; Rev.20:12).

The death of Hagar is never mentioned in scripture. Christ is the end of the law for righteousness to believers—He is not the end of the law. Much of it has not been fulfilled. It will go until every jot and tittle is fulfilled—likely forever.

The covenant of the law (Hagar), the scripture says, is "Mount Sinai." "Which things are an allegory: For these are the two covenants; the one from the mount Sinai, which gendereth to bondage, which is Agar" (Gal. 4:24). What happened there? The Ten Commandments, the moral law, came. Hagar, remember, was a servant. When Isaac was born, it was over for her. "But now we are delivered from the law, that being dead wherein we were held; that we would serve in newness of spirit, and not in the oldness of the letter" (Rom. 7:6). The apostle Paul, Christ's special messenger, says he is "dead to the law" (Gal. 2:19). Can we grasp this? What does it mean to be dead? All true believers are, in fact, dead to the law and alive to the resurrected Christ by the Holy Spirit. Then, let us take our freedom and exercise our grace-given power for holiness.

But now, some of Christendom, I fear, are in doldrums like a prisoner set free who won't leave the jail. Compare this story. There was a certain serviceman who had been freed from a German prison camp in World War II. He had been shot down during a B-17 bombing raid over Germany. Sitting with friends over lunch, a sudden rainstorm and a loud thunderclap roared. The serviceman, herein called Pilot, showed fear. He told this story. After his plane was shot down, Nazis captured and placed Pilot with other captured Americans in a prison camp next to an ammunition depot. Tons of explosives were stockpiled in the depot. Of course, the reason was so that Americans would not bomb the depot. They did not. But as the war moved on, the Russians approached from the east. The Russians had little concern for the prison camp.

One night, from miles away, they began cannon bombardment of the munitions depot. The prisoners, with their German guards, listened as the missiles flew near the depot and exploded. Fear reached hysteria. In the early hours of daylight, the German guards opened the doors of the prison, set the prisoners free, and told Pilot and the others they were fleeing to the American lines.

Pilot and his associates, still shaken with fear from the bombardment, went with them. They reached the American forces, who notified the Russians. The bombardment ceased. Pilot rejoiced. Freedom, clean clothes, and decent food.

The American forces went on to the prison and captured the munitions depot. And, in the prison, surprisingly, still sitting by their beds, were a few of the captured servicemen. As far as they were concerned, they were still in prison—yet with the prison doors open. Each moment, they had been in danger of being blown up by the Russian bombardment. So numb to their imprisonment were they that they could not accept freedom.

Are any such in Christendom? So used to the captivity of sin that they cannot accept their freedom in Christ?

The Jew is under the law written in tablets of stone. The Gentile, in nature, is under the works of the law written in conscience. But the believer is in Christ by faith in the gospel. Christ has fulfilled the law on our behalf, and He is now our "Man in Glory," as we who know God shall be too before long. We have this hope of eternal righteousness.

The Holy Spirit wrote the gospel in a one-sentence brief: "For I delivered unto you first of all that which I also received, how that Christ died for our sins according to the scriptures; And that he was buried, and that he rose again the third day according to the scriptures" (1 Cor. 15:3–4). So, too, did He record the law, as seen in the tenth chapter of Luke, in a one-sentence brief:

> He said unto him, "What is written in the law? How readest thou?" And he answering said, "thou shalt love the Lord thy God with all thy heart, and with all thy soul, and with all thy strength, and with all thy mind; and thy neighbor as thyself." And he said unto him, "Thou hast answered right: this do, and thou shalt live." (Luke 10:26–28)

No one except Christ has done that or can do that. For now, the Lord Jesus Christ fulfilled the law on the behalf of us who trust Him. The law says "do"; the gospel says "done."

May God give us all the wisdom and the discernment to submit ourselves to the righteousness of God! That is my prayer and purpose. Two roads: Isaac, the road of God's promise; Ishmael, the road of man's works.

CHAPTER 7

HIGHWAY ROBBERS

During a famine, Abraham's grandson (Jacob), with his sons and their families and servants, moved to Egypt for food. This move came about through the power of Jacob's son, Joseph. Joseph was sold into slavery but rose to the rank of what we would call the prime minister of Egypt. Then came a change of dynasty in Egypt. The new dynasty was hostile to Jacob's clan, called the Hebrews. Over the years, they multiplied into many people and by their very numbers seemed a threat to the Egyptians. Four hundred years passed. The Hebrew slaves degenerated. Many remembered but little the faith of their fathers and took on the idol worship of the Egyptians. Cruelty made them weak. But the Lord intervened as he had promised Abraham (Gen. 15:14).

Here is the way it began with the Lord in charge. The Lord called a man named Moses. Earlier, he was a prince in Pharaoh's house, reared by Pharaoh's daughter, yet the son of Hebrew slaves. The Lord called Moses when he was in exile from Egypt, serving as a herdsman with the Moabite people. The Lord gave Moses miraculous signs to show Pharaoh the power of Moses's demands. The basic demand was: let my people, the Hebrews, go free! The signs were, each one, a direct hit at the gods Pharaoh and the Egyptians worshipped. Their purpose: to show Pharaoh a warning of the Lord's superior power and the authority of the demand for Israel's freedom. The idols Pharaoh worshipped as gods seem foolish to us, but in his mind, they had great power. Moses's God, our Lord, if shown by Moses to be a supreme authority and power, could secure obedience from Pharaoh, an absolute monarch to the Egyptians, and secure freedom for the Hebrews.

But Satan had servants to obstruct: court magicians. I will call them "highway robbers" because they served to dull Pharaoh's fear of God and make Moses look as one having no demand warranting obedience. They, by mimicking Moses, robbed Pharaoh of his respect for God's word; they robbed Moses of his authority. Their ultimate purpose was to rob the millions of Hebrew slaves of their freedom; and through their opposition to God, rob Him of the fulfillment of His promise to Abraham.

Let's look at the story and see how these Egyptian magicians are a foreshadow, and also the type of people who would rob us on our journey to the eternal city.

Even before the birth of his son Ishmael, the Lord spoke to Abraham:

> And he said unto Abram, "Know of a surety that thy
> seed shall be a stranger in a land that is not theirs,
> and shall serve them; and they shall afflict them four
> hundred years; And also that nation, whom they
> shall serve, will I judge: and afterward shall they
> come out with great substance." (Gen. 15:13–14)

So it happened. Jacob (Israel) took his sons and servants and belongings to Egypt during a drought in his homeland. Pharaoh, the king, honored Israel. Jacob's son Joseph had become the prime minister of Egypt. But the political climate changed when a new king came to power. This Pharaoh, fearing the strength and numbers of the Israelites, forced them into slavery.

Some four hundred years passed. The Lord blessed Israel, despite their enslavement. He prepared one of them for leadership: Moses. Taken up from the Nile by Pharaoh's own daughter when he was a baby, Moses was reared in the royal palace. Pharaoh's daughter reared Moses as her own son. Moses could have enjoyed riches and station of power, but, in the prime of life, he chose to identify with his own people, Israel.

The Lord called Moses to lead Israel to freedom and their homeland. When He called Moses, He gave him miraculous signs to show Pharaoh, the king of Egypt, the power of God and that He had called Moses to bring the nation of Israel to freedom and their own land. The account is recorded in Exodus, chapters 5 through 10.

These signs were indeed miracles. They might seem irrelevant to us, but not so to Pharaoh. The Egyptians worshipped the

Nile River and the numerous animals surrounding it. They even worshipped its snakes and vermin. The first sign the Lord gave Moses was to cast his staff to the ground. It became a serpent. He took it up, and it became a staff.

Now, Moses and his brother, Aaron, are before Pharaoh. Moses demands that the Israelites be free to worship the Lord. Pharaoh asks for a sign. Aaron casts down his staff, and it becomes a serpent. But Satan, too, is on the scene, in the persons of the court magicians. They cast down their staffs, which, magically, become serpents. Aaron's serpent swallows up the magician's serpents, but Pharaoh's heart is hardened. He refuses to grant Israel's freedom. This scene is repeated with different signs Moses and Aaron give to Pharaoh, until, finally, the magicians are unable to replicate life by their craft. It is a miraculous creation: living lice from the dust. But the damage is done. Pharaoh is hardened and refuses to give freedom to the nation of Israel. He neither fears nor respects the Lord. The magicians were robbers. They robbed Pharaoh, the king, from his fear of God and respect for God's demands to "let my people go." God and His servant, Moses, and Israel, were also robbed and hindered, but not defeated. (Later, we shall see the picture of the gospel in the Passover judgment on Pharaoh and Egypt that brought freedom and riches to the Israelites, just as the Lord had promised Abraham.)

The magicians in Egypt who hindered freedom for God's people are a picture of false Christians who, now, by their false example, rob unbelievers of their respect for God and fear of His judgment:

> Having a form of godliness, but denying the power thereof: from such turn away. For of this sort are they which creep into houses, and lead captive silly women laden with sins, led away with divers lusts, Ever learning, and never able to come to the knowledge of the truth. Now as Jannes and Jambres withstood Moses, so do these also resist the truth: men of corrupt minds, reprobate concerning the faith. But they shall proceed no further: for their folly shall be manifest unto all men, as theirs also was. (2 Tim. 3:5–9)

The magicians could only pretend to do miracles, but Moses and Aaron acted by the power of God. For the magicians, it was an outward show. The scripture calls it a "form of godliness."

A Bible teacher recently spoke on the Gospel of John, third chapter, to a group in an established, recognized religious organization. An officer of the organization came to the teacher at the conclusion. "Why do you talk about being born again? I have been an officer here for twenty years, attended every Sunday. I have never heard about that before. Why do you talk about being born again?" The teacher responded, "Because the Lord Jesus Christ said, 'Ye must be born again;' and that is why I talk about it."

The forms of Christianity are beautiful: baptism and the Lord's Supper. But unless a person has the power of the Holy Spirit within, having been born again by the Spirit, they are, frankly, a sham. Without the power of God, one lives a life that hinders the work of the gospel in the world. Looking on the lives of such robs unbelievers of their respect and fear of God, which lead to repentance and faith.

Pharaoh, after a judgment of locusts on the land of Egypt, even went through a sham repentance from his sin:

> Then Pharaoh called for Moses and Aaron in haste; and he said, "I have sinned against the Lord your God, and against you. Now therefore forgive, I pray thee, my sin is only this once, and intreat the Lord your God, that he may take away from me this death only." (Exod. 10:16–17)

Pharaoh then turned back to his old sin, like a "dog to its vomit," and died in it.

Repentance from sin without faith in Jesus Christ proves useless. There is no power in it; just as Pharaoh hardened his heart, going back to his old ways. No one who repents without faith really does repent. Judas himself "repented" after betraying Christ. He even took the thirty pieces of silver paid to him for pointing out Christ for his arrest and then tried to make restitution by giving it back, after which he hanged himself and went "to his own place." Tragically, when God's law has done its good works in the heart of a person who becomes under conviction, today's highway robbers, as did Pharaoh's magicians, point not to faith in Christ but to some religious works of their own glory.

Nature illustrates. The impala of Africa approach a water hole warily. A cheetah or leopard may be lurking there. They become frightened at the rustling of the wind in the grass, and go bounding off. The sound is like a pride of lions approaching to attack. But there is an enemy they seem to accept without fear. This enemy moves among them frequently; it even seems to protect and befriend them. It never rushes upon them, never chases them; it just waits until there is a newborn and then eats it. This enemy is their seeming friend, the baboon.

These "magicians" appear outwardly to be friendly Christians, but, because of their own pride and desire to rule, they turn young Christians to their own ways of outward religion that masks unholy living and sham repentance. True repentance is toward God and faith toward the Lord Jesus Christ (Acts 20:21). God is no taskmaster like Pharaoh. God is love. God frees people from the slavery of sin, gives joy to the heart and a true hope for the coming of Christ and the promise of everlasting life in His eternal kingdom.

Some entire organizations have nothing but a form of godliness. That is in their doctrine. They neither have nor know of anything else. Is there any chance for such? Jesus said, "If any man will do his will, he shall know of the doctrine, whether it be of God, or whether I speak of myself" (John 7:17). Yes, there is. Many examples abound. Martin Luther, for example. Here is a scriptural promise for such: "And of some have compassion, making a difference: And others save with fear, pulling them out of the fire; hating even the garment spotted by the flesh" (Jude 22–23). This passage is directed to persons not knowing the truth but wanting to know.

Here is a story about a brave and honest Realtor, disabled, who was taught only that the way to eternal life was to keep the Ten Commandments. Being convicted by the Spirit, he knew he had not, and knew he was without hope of eternal life, but having been taught nothing else, he became hostile to religion. Then, how God opened his mind, and he heard and believed the gospel, found freedom and assurance of eternal salvation before he passed from this life.

A man, herein called Buyer, found the vacant lot on which he wanted to build a house. This lot was listed with a broker. His neighbor, a Christian, herein called Friend, knowing this, came to him with this request concerning one we will call Brother. Brother had been a successful Realtor, but a stroke made him disabled, barely able to move about with crutches. "If you will let him come in on the deal," said Friend, "he can, as your agent, help you and can get a commission from the broker. In fact, he will come in for half the usual commission and will be able to lower the final price with the broker that much, saving you a good bit of money." Buyer and Brother agreed.

Brother met with Buyer at the property and afterwards. He made helpful suggestions for the purchase. On his crutches, he bravely examined the wooded lot to be purchased. Grossly handicapped, Brother never complained, although the stroke had cost him his health, his business, and his standing in the community, and placed his family in financial straits. Buyer, a believer, did not mention anything about the scripture or the way of salvation because Friend had told him of Brother's feelings. "Brother," he said, "will not talk about the Bible.

He believes in God's law. If you keep it, you go to heaven. If you don't, you go to hell. He says he hasn't kept it, and can't keep it, so he is not going to heaven and will not talk about it—even to me. Best not mention it." So, Buyer didn't mention it.

Buyer and Brother, together, visited the broker and got a good offer of sale for the lot in question. They left broker's office and went for a close examination of the lot before signing the contract. On the way, an unseen One spoke to Buyer, almost audibly, saying, "Give him a full commission, not half." Whereupon Buyer told Brother, "I am going to pay you a full commission, not half, on the deal." Brother refused and said, "A deal is a deal. I made a deal with you for half a commission, and that is the way it will have to be." Buyer replied, "No, you will take a full commission, or I will not sign with the broker and I will not buy the property." Brother responded, "Well, if you put it that way, I have no choice. I will take the full commission." Buyer said, "Fine." They returned to the broker's office, and Buyer signed the contract. On the way home, riding together, Brother spoke up, saying, "I will be glad to get the full commission. My family really needs the money."

Sometime later, after purchasing the lot, Buyer met Friend, who gave him unsettling news about Brother. He was suffering from a fast-acting cancer and had a life expectancy of only a few weeks. Friend told him, "He will not talk with me at all about the Bible. I have tried. The fellow who lives next door is a deacon in the church and has tried to talk with him. Brother refuses to talk with him, even though they are good friends. Will you try to talk with him about Christ? He likes you."

Of course, Buyer would make an attempt. He phoned Brother's home. Brother's wife answered. Buyer said, "I would like to come by and talk with your husband about salvation in Christ. Do you think he would let me come?" To his surprise, which made him tremble, this is what Brother's wife replied: "Yes, he will let you come. He told me he knew you would come. He will be waiting for you."

When Buyer arrived, Brother was sitting at a table, waiting. Buyer showed him from the scripture that Christ, who was sinless, was made to be sin on the cross for us, fulfilling the law's demands; that Christ is the end of the law for righteousness to all who believe; that God raised Him from the dead, accepting His payment for our sins, where Christ, now alive in glory, is the giver of our righteousness.

Brother agreed, accepted, and asked Christ to come into his heart, and thanked Him for salvation. A short time later, Brother passed away, but in the meantime, he gave confession repeatedly that he had eternal life in Christ and knew he was going to heaven when he died.

The Spirit convicted Brother, and he responded. Before being saved, he dealt in the truth about his condition, and his honest work brought him to the light. "For every one that doeth evil hateth the light, neither cometh to the light, lest his deeds should be reproved. But he that doeth truth cometh to the light, that his deeds may be made manifest, that they are wrought in God" (John 3:20–21).

True, there are highway robbers, but there is a warrant for their arrest—called the gospel—which will stop their work and give seekers entry to the road to glory.

CHAPTER 8

A FEAST TO REMEMBER

Often we observe celebrations with a great meal. Sometimes we repeat a journey, in part, because of a special feast at a particular restaurant. There is a feast that our Jewish friends (Israelites) have remembered for more than thirty-five hundred years: Passover. It is a memorial we can enjoy on the road to glory because it has a special meaning for us who know God, believing in His Son, the Lord Jesus Christ.

Here is how it all began. Moses, the Lord's servant, prophesied judgment after Pharaoh, Egypt's ruler, had denied freedom to the Israelites. And so it came to pass against Pharaoh and all the Egyptians. In all the plagues that came upon Egypt, the Israelites alone suffered nothing in their persons or property. These things came upon Egypt. The Nile River, upon which they depended for food, vomited up its fish, dead and stinking. Frogs and lice covered the land. Flies swarmed everywhere, even in Pharaoh's palace. Running sores broke out on the cattle, horses, camels, and sheep.

Pharaoh pretended to change his mind, but then he continued to harden his heart. Hail smote the land, destroying the flax and barley. Locusts swarmed on the fields.

Even Pharaoh's staff rebuked him, saying, "How long shall this man be a snare unto us? Let the men go that they may serve the Lord their God: Knowest thou not yet that Egypt is destroyed" (Exod. 10:7). All because Pharaoh grasped greedily to keep a people slaves to build monuments to his greatness.

After Pharaoh tried more compromises on Moses, unsuccessfully, more judgment came: total darkness over Egypt for three days. Pharaoh attempted one last compromise: "Go ye, serve the Lord; only let your flocks and your herds be stayed." Again, Moses refused: "Our cattle also shall go with us; there shall not a hoof be left behind ..." Pharaoh, with his heart hardened, said, "Get thee from me, take heed to thyself, see my face no more; for in that day thou sees my face, thou shalt die." And Moses said, "Thou has spoken well. I will see thy face again no more" (Exod. 10:28–29).

We come now to the most important celebration of the Israelite people. It is kept today, in reduced form, as the most important time in the Jewish calendar: Passover. It is the type and the foreshadow of our Lord's sacrifice on the cross. Just as this event brought freedom from slavery in Egypt to Israel, now, fulfilled in Christ's sacrifice, does it bring freedom from the penalty and slavery of sin to the believer—and more, much more.

The Lord had told Abraham his descendants would come forth with much substance. After the Passover event, the Egyptians gave their treasures to the Israelites—so anxious were the Egyptians to see the Israelites depart.

Now, let us look at Passover and its successor (to us believers): the Lord's Supper. As we remember, it becomes feast of feasts and the nourishment of our souls. The apostle Paul says, "Christ our Passover is sacrificed for us" (1 Cor. 5:7). On the cross, Christ died for our sins.

It is called Passover because the Lord smote the firstborn of man and beast with death in Egypt, without exception, unless there was blood of a lamb or a goat—as He had proscribed—on the posts and over the doorway of the dwelling. The Israelites followed the proscription, and the Lord passed over their dwellings.

Here is the record of this ordinance, the Lord speaking to Moses:

> "Your lamb shall be without blemish, a male of the first year: ye shall take it out from the sheep, or from the goats: And ye shall keep it up until the fourteenth day of the same month: and the whole assembly of the congregation of Israel shall kill it in the evening. And they shall take of the blood,

and strike it on the two side posts and on the upper door post of the houses, wherein they shall eat it. And they shall eat the flesh in that night, roast with fire, and unleavened bread; and with bitter herbs they shall eat it. Eat not of it raw, nor sodden at all with water, but roast with fire; his head with his legs, and with the purtenance thereof. And ye shall let nothing of it remain until the morning; and that which remaineth of it until the morning ye shall burn with fire. And thus shall ye eat it; with your loins girded, your shoes on your feet, and your staff in your hand; and ye shall eat it in haste; it is the Lord's Passover. For I will pass through the land of Egypt this night, and will smite all the firstborn in the land of Egypt, both man and beast; and against all the gods of Egypt I will execute judgment: I am the Lord. And the blood shall be to you for a token upon the houses where ye are: and when I see the blood, I will pass over you and the plague shall not be upon you to destroy you, when I smite the land of Egypt. And this day shall be unto you for a memorial; and ye shall keep it a feast to the Lord throughout your generations; ye shall keep it a feast by an ordinance forever." (Exod. 12:5–14)

Now, Christ crucified is our Passover.

Remember Jesus was a law-abiding Jew. On the night before Passover, at the preparation meal, he instituted what is called the Lord's Supper. With him in the upper room of a friend's home were eleven of his chosen apostles. Judas Iscariot, the betrayer, had left to confirm his bargain to point out Jesus at night to his enemies, so they could arrest Him apart from the many people who loved Him.

Judas, committed, could not repent or retreat.

To trap a fox, a metal sleeve with a little chick at the base of it is placed in the ground. The fox goes in the sleeve to catch the chick, and then the fox cannot back out. Trapped! Just so, Judas, having betrayed "the innocent blood of Christ" could not get out of the trap. Beware! Lest Satan get in a box with no escape the one who refuses Christ.

From the scriptures, we read:

> "The Son of man indeed goeth, as it is written of him; but woe to that man by whom the Son of man is betrayed! Good were it for that man if he had never been born." And as they did eat, Jesus took bread, and blessed, and brake it, and gave to them and said, "Take, eat: this is my body." And he took the cup, and when he had given thanks, he gave it to them, and they all drank of it. And he said unto them, "This is my blood of the new testament, which is shed for many. Verily, I say unto you, I will drink no more of the fruit of the vine, until that day that I drink it new in the kingdom of God." (Mark 14:21–25)

That dark night, Jesus was unlawfully arrested; unlawfully tried before an unlawful makeshift court; then taken to King Herod, where He was tormented and mocked with thorns on His head. On the following day, he was taken to Pontius Pilate, Roman governor of the Jewish nation. Here, a hired mob demanded the hideous form of Roman execution, shouting, "Crucify Him." This mob, a claque for the politicians who hated Jesus, packed the courtroom, screaming, and intimidated the Roman governor, whereupon, he, in a coward's gesture, sentenced our Lord to death on the cross. This was on the fourteenth of Nisan, the first month of the Jewish religious calendar.

While the high priest plunged the knife into Israel's sacrificial lamb for Israel to eat the Passover, the Roman soldiers pounded nails into the hands and feet of our Lord, who surrendered Himself as God's sacrificial lamb. (For a detailed account, see John 13:1–2, 18:28, 19:31.)

The feast of Passover, which the Lord gave Moses as the prophetic word, is now fulfilled. As a foreshadow, it repeats and expands the theme of the gospel message in graphic representation.

Fortunately, for Jew and gentile alike, while on the cross, Jesus prayed, "Forgive them for they know not what they do." Had they known, they would not have crucified the Lord of glory. That prayer for forgiveness has been answered and comes down to us like an entitlement if we will accept it by faith.

Let us notice from the text certain facts relating to Passover and the way in which they are fulfilled in God's Christ and our Savior. Remember Jesus said, "Search the Scriptures; for in them ye think ye have eternal life: and they are they which testify of me" (John 5:39).

As to the Passover: The lamb was without blemish. Jesus lived a sinless life. No sin haunted His nature. No lust of the flesh caused Him to stumble. There was no shadow on His walk with God, nor did He have any mistakes to confess. It has been said that He is as much God as though not man and as much man as though not God. At Jesus's so-called trial, Pilate, revealing far more than he knew, said, "I find no fault in him" (John 19:4).

As a lamb gives no resistance when taken, so did our Lord offer Himself up to his killers. A picture of His crucifixion between two thieves shows the thieves with their arms and legs bound to the cross, but no binding on the Savior. Historically true or not, the picture shows that Christ offered Himself up. The body would naturally have convulsed and pulled away when being nailed. Binding to the cross would be necessary to keep the hands and feet steady for nailing. Jesus allowed His crucifixion. He, the eternal Son of God "by whom and for whom all things consist," could have, in a word, spoken His killers into the dust of the earth.

Obedient Israel roasted and ate the sacrificial lamb, with their shoes on, ready to depart to their promised land. They ate the Passover sacrifice with bitter herbs. When the Lord is calling one into the kingdom of God on this earth, He convicts of sin, "because they believe not on me." Bitter herbs.

When God saved me, conviction of sin struck me like a knife in the center of my body, and I lay down on the floor. I saw, for the first time, my spiritual problem. It was not simply wrongdoing. I was a wrongdoer and away from God in continual and total violation of His law. I was headed for His judgment. To be acceptable to God, I needed to receive the Lord Jesus Christ by faith.

Some will not repent toward God, fearing the journey before them. Others will not start the journey of faith because they hold on to some idol, or to love of sin, like a monkey with its hand caught in a trap. The monkey trap is a hole large enough for a monkey to pull out its hand alone, but not large enough for it to pull out its hand holding the piece of fruit at the bottom of the hole. The monkey holds on to the fruit, taking capture rather than letting go. It complains loudly, but its sense of priority isn't good. Sadly, there are people, who, because of hanging on to something of this world, never start on the road to glory.

From reading the New Testament, it appears to me that the biggest idol people in biblical times—and perhaps even now—hang on to, refusing to let go of it and accept Christ, is self-righteousness, with its many religious symbols and liturgies. May God grant such to be the beneficiaries of the Lord's prophecy: "And ye shall know the truth, and the truth shall make you free" (John 8:32).

The Israelites ate all of the lamb. Any leftover was burned—nothing left behind. Here is a hint of the resurrection of Jesus. When His friends came to the cave where His body, wrapped in burial bindings, had been placed, so they could anoint His body, it was not there. It was gone. Later, the apostle looked in the empty tomb, saw what had been the Lord's burial bindings still wrapped like the cocoon of a pupa but no body within it, and in his heart believed the resurrection of his Lord. Had the body of the Lord been taken up by another, the bindings would not have been there undisturbed. (John 20:8–9)

The judgment of death comes for dwellings not under the blood, on the eldest offspring of every family in Egypt, without exception, on the first Passover—Egyptian or Israelite. The eldest, of course, represents the entire family. The witness: all die eternally who have not the blood of God's Lamb, Jesus Christ, sprinkled on the heart, as on God's throne in heaven, for sin. For us, it is the death of Christ taken by faith, or death as a sinner. "The soul that sinneth shall die." Based on the judgment of Passover, the Egyptians thrust out the Israelites with Egypt's treasures. Israel was free to go. Moses led. They followed, with a cloud before them, to the Red Sea by faith. The sea opened up a wall on either side. The Spirit of God was in control, and they all passed through the sea, out of Egypt and onto dry ground.

Pharaoh cringed at his loss of slaves. He turned back to his love of power, and, with his army, he pursued the Israelites. The floor of the sea cracked open underneath the weight of his chariots; the wall of water on each side collapsed. He died in the sea. (Exod. 13–14)

Here is a striking picture of the believer's freedom from slavery of sin and the strength of sin—the law. Passing through the sea to freedom was a miracle. Likewise, the new birth of one accepting Christ by faith is a miracle. It is a work of the Holy Spirit and puts one beyond the dominance of sinful flesh and death, with a new dominant nature given by God—a nature that loves holiness and hates sin. The nature of sin is still present and ready to attack, as we shall see, but it is no longer in control.

The cloud went before Israel. In darkness it was light; in light it was darkness. As Israel went through the sea, walled up on either side, the cloud was a fire of light overhead. Pharaoh, following with his army, saw a dark cloud. The cloud, of course, was a theophany, a divine manifestation.

What is light to the believer in the gospel message is darkness to the one outside Christ. As the apostle Paul tells us:

> Which things also we speak, not in the words which man's wisdom teacheth, but which the Holy Ghost teacheth; comparing spiritual things with spiritual. But the natural man receiveth not the things of the Spirit of God: for they are foolishness unto him: neither can he know them, because they are spiritually discerned. (1 Cor. 2:13–14)

The Passover had a testimony to "strangers," people in Egypt outside the faith. The Passover was eaten in the homes of God's people in Egypt and, later, in the Jewish nation. The stranger could see this. The stranger could not partake unless he or she joined the covenant ranks. Then, the stranger could partake of Passover and, in fact, was counted as a full member of the faith.

The gospel message takes this to the next step: The fulfilling of the Passover, in prophecy, can and should be shared with unbelievers, who, accepting Christ, have full benefits of everlasting life on the road to glory. Thus, the stranger is a stranger no more. The natural man is now spiritual, and the door to spiritual things is open. Unfortunately, there is a proud arrogance in much of urban life. Humanism and naturalism are, it seems, the order of the day. Indeed, there is a "famine of hearing the word." However, if we look, we can still find people with an open mind and a teachable attitude in matters of the spirit and eternal life.

God required the celebration of the Passover to be repeated (Exod. 12:14). It had prime importance to Israel. Its message still has prime importance to all because the sacrifice of the Passover is fulfilled by the sacrifice of Christ on the cross.

Believers now have the ordinance of the Lord's Supper. Jesus said, "This do in remembrance of me." It pictures the fulfillment of Passover: His body broken for us, and His blood shed for the remission of sins. As John the Baptist said, "behold the Lamb of God which taketh away the sin of the world." The gospel saves us, the scripture says, if kept in memory, "by which also ye are saved, if ye keep in memory" (1 Cor. 15:2). We are kept by faith—not out of it. I have found my natural mind is tempted and tends to go back to a leaning on work's righteousness for standing before God. The repetition of the gospel message and the warning to "keep in memory" thwarts this temptation.

When I was a child, our family grew sweet corn in a garden. Mother put it up in sealed jars. It kept. On occasion, the corn in one of the jars would swell and turn blue at the top. It wasn't sealed. It wasn't kept. In fact, Mother warned us to never eat such corn. "It is very poisonous," she said.

Some of the most vicious people I have known claimed to have been saved by Christ. But they were not being kept. They were poisonous and not sealed. But mankind is not corn and not without a will. We have a sense of responsibility.

All of us need to remember the scripture message that is both a promise and a warning: "How shall we escape, if we neglect so great salvation; which at the first began to be spoken by the Lord and was confirmed unto us by them that heard him" (Heb. 2:3).

When we Christians feast on what the Lord has done for us, we would do well to remember our debt to Israel. God used them to preserve and write the scriptures. They made up the first churches. Indeed, there is now a remnant among them who know and have accepted Messiah, our Lord Jesus. True, they are a mystery, a "treasure hid in a field": "Again, the kingdom of heaven is like unto treasure hid in a field; the which when a man hath found, he hideth, and for joy thereof goeth and selleth all that he hath, and buyeth that field" (Matt. 13:44). Among them, as noted in the scriptures, are Nicodemus and Joseph of Arimathea (John 19:38–39). There is reason to believe the unlawful meeting of the Sanhedrin (Jewish court) at night, when they delivered Jesus of Nazareth to the Romans to be crucified, was without notice on purpose: to keep Nicodemus and Joseph out. If present, they would not have tolerated the Sanhedrin's actions. It was Joseph, with Nicodemus's help, who reverently placed Jesus's body in his own tomb, in a garden. There, it was sealed by Rome with a great stone and guarded by soldiers.

God's angel rolled away the stone, not that Jesus needed it removed to come out, but so his disciples could see the tomb was empty and testify to His bodily resurrection.

Now we believers sit at His table and feast on the meaning of Passover: Christ crucified for our sins, delivering us from the slavery of sin. At the other end of the table are ones who were before us and who still are present—the Jewish remnant:

> God hath not cast away his people which he foreknew. Wot ye not what the scripture saith of Elias? how he maketh intercession to God against Israel, saying, "Lord, they have killed thy prophets, and digged down thine altars; and I am left alone, and they seek my life." But what saith the answer of God unto him? "I have reserved to myself seven thousand men, who have not bowed the knee to the image of Baal." Even so then at this present time also there is a remnant according to the election of grace. (Rom. 11:2–5)

Here is a story that came to me from a true source. It gives a hint of the "treasure hid in a field"—the remnant—strangers to us, perhaps, but not to God. Nor are they strangers on the road—believers who are Jews.

The waiting room of the state prison for youth is almost empty. A receptionist sits at her desk, reading in quiet, but it is the quiet of anticipation because it is Christmastime. Inside an adjoining office suite is a secretary at her desk, and a deputy sheriff stands by. Next is the office of the warden, who sits talking with his wife. They are waiting for the honored guest of the day: a benefactor, herein called Benny. Benny has supported the warden politically and professionally. Being a generous man, Benny, the proprietor of a chain of department stores, provides clothing and shoes, free of charge for everyone, upon the warden's requisition, so that "the defendant doesn't have to go to court in rags." Each year, Benny provides Christmas dinner for the hundreds of inmates of the prison, the warden's prison staff, and the families of the prisoners and the staff. The Christmas dinner is catered. It is a banquet without ceiling of cost. Benny arrives at the time expected. He and the warden, with the warden's wife and a deputy sheriff, leave the office suite and go next door to a large gymnasium where Christmas festivities have already begun. Jolly music fills the air. Roasted turkey, cranberry sauce, oyster dressing, hot vegetables, breads, and apple and pumpkin pies are being wheeled through the security doors and into the gym, to food stations located on the floor in front of the bleachers. Sitting on the bleachers with prison staff are the prisoners and their families. The prisoners have earned this privilege in a behavior-modification program, with points given for daily good behavior.

The warden, his wife, Benny, and the deputy sheriff take reserved seats in the center of the bleacher directly in front of a stage located on the other side of the gym. After greetings to those thereabout, the warden excuses himself to go about greeting the families of prison staff members, leaving his wife and Benny in pleasant conversation.

A brief program begins. The prison athletic director, a member of the Fellowship of Christian Athletes, previously asked the warden for time for a brief program on stage by Christian athletes during the dinner setup. The warden approved the request.

Christmas carols come on the loudspeakers. Then comes a speaker, an internationally famous professional hockey player. His face is scarred. With his huge hands gesturing, he begins to preach. It reminds the warden of how he imagined John the Baptist to have preached. The hockey player preaches the virgin birth of Jesus, the promised Jewish Messiah; Jesus's sinless life; His betrayal by Judas to Jewish leaders; His substitutionary death in our place on the cross; His bodily resurrection; His imminent coming again to establish His kingdom on earth.

And, further, the hockey player warns, "Unless you repent of your way of life and believe in Jesus, God's Son, you will die in your sins and burn forever in a devil's hell."

The hockey player continues in this mode. The prisoners and their families listen intently. The warden is surprised at such blunt speech and looks at Benny. He knows that Benny is a member and leader of a large conservative Jewish synagogue. And Benny, while the hockey player is preaching, is standing and shouting something in return, slapping his hands together—surprising to the warden, because Benny is not ordinarily excitable.

The warden thinks to himself, *Benny is Jewish. This sermon is upsetting him. He will end the annual Christmas dinner for this prison.* And he goes to stand by Benny.

To the warden's amazement, he hears what Benny is saying and repeating as he stands, slapping his hands together. Benny says, "Isn't that wonderful! Isn't that wonderful! Isn't that wonderful!"

Then it comes to the warden's understanding. The religious calendar and celebration on certain days is important to Jews. Benny's provision each year for the prison's Christmas celebration, celebrating the birth of Christ, is his way of confessing: "I, too, believe in Jesus of Nazareth, the Messiah, the Lord Jesus Christ." His financial support continued.

Benny is gone from this life now, but the warden looks forward to seeing him at the end of the road to glory.

One day, when Christ returns, the treasure hidden in the field will be brought forth out of the field and "all Israel will be saved."

CHAPTER 9

INTO THE WAR ZONE

The Lord, by Moses, led Israel past the Red Sea on the way to the promised land. The Lord knew Amalekites, descendants of Jacob's brother, Esau, would attack them to destroy them. He knows the end from the beginning, so He prepared His people by the discipline that discipline brings.

Hardship attended Israel's way: hunger, thirst, and labor. Unfortunately, the nation complained. Hardship will attend our way on the road to glory. Consider the words of Paul and Barnabas, spoken to the new believers: "Exhorting them to continue in the faith and that we must through much tribulation enter into the Kingdom of God" (Acts 14:22). But, unlike an attack by Satan, which would destroy us, God's chastisement has, in its result, more faith and strength of character, which prepare us for our role as priests and kings. "And hath made us kings and priests unto God and His father; to him be the glory and dominion ever and ever. Amen" (Rev. 1:6). Every one of the troubles that the Lord allows has a good outcome, and the cheer of His presence is with us to guide us.

What happened to Aunt Lila is an illustration. Her grandfather liked her and told everyone, "Lila is my favorite." He passed away and, although a poor farmer, left a will. In the will, he bequeathed: "To my granddaughter, Lila, the black iron pot in the front closet that has the old magazines on it." No other bequest came to Lila. She kept the iron pot with old magazines on it because she loved her grandfather, but she was hurt, thinking he really didn't care for her at all.

One day, she decided to remove the old magazines and clean up the old pot. To her joy, she found under the magazines fifty hundred-dollar bills. It was all the savings her grandfather had and, at that time, was a fortune that would buy a nice house. The disappointments for us on the road to glory carry a hidden treasure.

By tradition, in old times, the Irish kings did not bring up their sons in opulence. Rather, they placed them in the custody of a trusted warrior and his family to learn discipline. One day, we, His children, will be in the road no longer; rather, we will have a kingdom to rule with the King of kings, our Lord Jesus Christ.

Before long on their journey to the promised land, the attack came on the Israelites:

> Then came Amalek, and fought with Israel in Pephidim. And Moses said unto Joshua, "Choose us out men; and go out, fight with Amalek; tomorrow I will stand on the top of the hill with the rod of God in mine hand." So Joshua did as Moses had said to him, and fought with Amalek; and Moses, Aaron and Hur went up to the top of the hill. And it came to pass, when Moses held up his hand, that Israel prevailed: and when he let down his hand, Amalek prevailed. But Moses' hand were heavy and they took a stone, and put it under him, and he sat thereon; and Aaron and Hur stayed up his hands, the one on the one side, and the other on the other side; and his hands were steady until the going down of the sun. And Joshua discomfited Amalek and his people with the edge of the sword. And the Lord said unto Moses, "Write this for a memorial in a book, and rehearse it in the ears of Joshua: for I will utterly put out the remembrance of Amalek from under heaven." (Exod. 17:8–14)

There are lessons for us to learn. Joshua, commanding Israel's armies, won the battle on earth with the sword—or so it would have appeared. He did what he could. The real victory was won, not where men were fighting with their weapons, but, rather, on the mountain where Moses lifted his arms in prayer. We have an advocate. The scripture tells us that Jesus, at the right hand of God, alive and in the heavens, is our lawyer, attending to our concerns. "Wherefore he is able also to save them to the uttermost that come unto God by him, seeing he ever liveth to make intercession for them" (Heb. 7:25).

But, here, we must resist the spiritual enemy. Joshua took up the sword, and we must resist with the sword: the Word of God used by faith.

When Satan attacks, we have an Advocate. We must not hesitate, but go to Jesus, our resurrected Lord, immediately.

There are times in life when the problems of life simply overwhelm us. We are simply so overcome that we feel we have no strength to even resist. These are the times when we must simply cast ourselves on the Lord in faith.

A rainstorm of greatness fell on a little village. The roadway in front of a small white house became a rushing river. A small boy, Jack, and his sister came out of the house as the rain stopped and came to the side of the rushing river that had been the roadway.

Jack waded in up to his knees and saw he was about to be thrown down by the strength of the current. He shouted back to his sister, "Don't come in. It is too deep. Run and get help. I am about to get washed away." His sister ran to the house to get her mother to come with a rope to toss to her brother. It was too late. Jack dived as hard as he could to the bank of the roadway. He almost made it, but the current was too strong. A mighty rush of higher water had come along from the hill above and completely submerged him, dragging him along the bottom of the roadway, on the way to a storm sewer one hundred feet below.

Jack could not swim; he could not get out. All he could do was to hold one arm up as he washed downstream on his side.

Now, the Lord knew this was going to happen. A neighbor, Mr. Beerbohm, a retired farmer, had come to the edge of the rushing water. Never such a rain had so made a river out of the roadway, and he saw, washing along the edge of the current, a hand sticking out of the water. Mr. Beerbohm got on his knees and reached out as far as he could, grabbed the hand, and pulled Jack to safety. There is a lesson here. When we are overwhelmed on the road to glory, we are to do what we can and surrender the matter to the Lord. He knows what is going on, and He is there to help.

Had Jack been more watchful, he would not have waded into the water. He would have seen the force of the water from the debris it carried. Jesus told the disciplines to "watch and pray."

When we watch, at times, we can even turn defeat into a victory, as Joshua and Moses did when attacked by Amalek.

I confess here an opportunity I missed simply by not being watchful.

My wife, Frances, and I had been on a cruise in the Caribbean. We had read of an Indian tribe and their ancient practice of blood sacrifice of their children and heroes to their demon god. We visited the magnificent remains of their otherwise-advanced culture. Our guide was a figure of grandeur. He was tall, handsome, witty, and erudite. In fact, many people from other tours joined our group because of our guide's ability to explain the architecture and customs of the people. He claimed to be an active priest of the very tribe. Perhaps he was.

He brought his followers, tourists all, to a certain mound. There he muttered some words and in authority commanded all of us to follow his lead in words of prayer to his demon god. Frances and I did not. Most, if not all, of the other tourists did as he said.

Out of the large gathering—hundreds of people—the guide watched and saw that I had not repeated his prayer after him as he commanded. The guide rudely singled me out. He pointed at me, ordered me to repeat after him his prayer, and asked me why I had not.

I was so surprised, I stood dumbfounded. I was not watchful. Here was an opportunity of a lifetime to speak up and witness for my God, and tell the guide and the tourists—most of whom would have agreed with me—that I prayed only to God and the Son of God Lord Jesus Christ. I could have turned his attack into a victory for the Lord. But, not being watchful, I simply stood there in dumb silence.

The guide, then thinking, I suppose, that my wife and I would follow his lead, led the whole assembly once again in the same prayer to his demon god. We still remained silent, and the guide moved on to another spot for his explanations, but the moment had gone.

This bothered me so much that I scheduled the same cruise at once when back home; we went on it. I wanted the opportunity for this guide to repeat, giving me such an opportunity again, but he was no longer employed as a guide. My opportunity to win a battle for the Lord was gone, and gone forever.

Another point. The apostle Paul knew Satan's tactics. He knew that we would feel so guilty after a failure that Satan would tempt us to cease our active participation in God's work. There was a couple in the church at Corinth who had engaged in an immoral union. Paul warned them. They repented. Paul knew that unless the church showed them forgiveness, the couple would have feelings of guilt brought on by Satan, the accuser, making them to be worthless in their service. Here is what Paul says concerning the repentant:

> So that contrariwise ye ought rather to forgive him, and comfort him, lest perhaps such a one should be swallowed up with overmuch sorrow. Wherefore I beseech you that ye would confirm your love toward him. For to this end also did I write that I might know the proof of you, whether ye be obedient in all things. To whom ye forgive any thing, I forgive also: for if I forgave any thing to whom I forgave it, for your sakes forgave I it in the person of Christ; Lest Satan should get an advantage of us: for we are not ignorant of his devices. (2 Cor. 2:7–11)

We are protected when we know Satan's methods.

There was a certain small young woman, Stella, a cousin of a Scottish laird, who, with her young husband, went as pioneers to the Dakota territory after the Civil War ended. She was an enterprising person and studied the customs of the Sioux tribes, comparing them to Scottish customs.

Her husband, called Pap, had been to what is now South Dakota and had secured a ranch with cattle: Spanish cattle from Texas mixed with Herefords to upgrade the herd. He had built, with his helpers, a sod house and outbuildings of sod. This was to be home. Pap returned for his bride, Stella. This young couple, by train and a covered wagon, ventured forth and began their lives as pioneer ranchers. All went well. The cattle prospered; the garden near the house, irrigated by a flowing stream, produced an abundance.

Then, one day, trouble came. Pap, with hired hands, was out tending cattle. Stella was alone in the sod cabin putting up cucumbers for the winter. A rider on a lathered horse rode up to the cabin. Stella invited him in. "I can't stop," he said. "I've got to ride on and warn the others. Indians are coming. They have burned out and killed and scalped some already. They are on the warpath. Tell Pap if you can." And he rode on at a gallop. Stella was alone. She breathed a prayer and then knew the Lord was with her. She remembered the ancient rule of hospitality: "you shall not harm a host while a guest and you shall not harm a guest."

A few minutes later, Stella saw mounted, painted, Indians crossing the stream toward her sod house. They had painted their faces and streaked their horses with a white clay that had deposits in South Dakota. They were on the warpath to kill, scalp, and burn. They had painted their bodies and horses so they would be beautiful in the happy hunting ground if killed on the warpath.

Stella could have boarded up the cabin and hid, or tried to run. She did not. She knew the rule of the Sioux—the same rule held in ancient Scotland—the rule of hospitality. She opened the windows. She opened the door. She took in her apron a full load of cucumbers in one arm and, going outside her door, waved the other arm in invitation to the Indians. "Come in and eat," she cried. They must have understood her sign, if not her words, because she gave them cucumbers, and they came in, gorged themselves until they got sick, took her present of more cucumbers, dumped them into the stream, and left Stella in peace. Neighbors were murdered or, if they escaped to safety, burned out. Not Pap and Stella. She was alive and their property safe because she knew the law of hospitality and used it—and the Indians on the warpath obeyed.

When we know the rule of God's hospitality and have confessed our sins as believers, and Satan accuses us to destroy us, our sins are gone. "If we confess our sins, he is faithful and just to forgive our sins, and to cleanse us from all unrighteousness" (1 John 1:9). Satan may try to burn our conscience with old sins, forgiven ones, but, as seen with David (Ps. 51) and Paul (Rom. 7:15), admitting them and confessing to God will drive him off. In any event, this line of attack by Satan is serious warfare and is not game playing. If not addressed, it can lead to depression and thoughts of suicide that will deplete our service to the Lord. Confession, even repeatedly if necessary, as with David (Ps. 51:3), can bring cleansing from all unrighteousness, including the weak faith that made one vulnerable to attack. Then the joy of salvation is restored, and the accusing thoughts on the warpath of the conscience that came to burn go away.

The battle is ours to win.

Here is an account of safety in a war zone. It is about a soldier, we will call Tim Pheiffer, and his protection while in danger.

There is power in prayer for protection of loved ones. Miracles of faith happen on the distant battlefield as well as at home.

It was an April morning in Kabul, Afghanistan. Captain Tim Pheiffer and two staff, one an interpreter, had come in from visiting mountain tribes to make report at the national police headquarters. Next to it was the embassy of India; like most Kabul buildings, it was a drab, gray, concrete structure.

After making their report, they signed out at 10:20 a.m.

Captain Pheiffer and staff went through security and to the police parking lot, got into their Humvee, and drove through the gate to their base—five miles away. They arrived at base some fifteen minutes later. When they arrived, they were met with shock, then with relief, and then with joy from their comrades. Here is why.

At 10:21 a.m., a member of the Taliban drove a truck loaded with explosives to the compound of the Indian embassy, and detonated.

The explosion destroyed the Indian embassy and blew down the gate and damaged the national police headquarters.

The troops at the base were surprised and joyful when Pheiffer and staff returned because it was believed they'd been destroyed in the blast. They knew Pheiffer signed out at 10:20 a.m.; but Pheiffer and staff had tried, after leaving the police headquarters, to report in again, but strangely the radio, operational until then, wouldn't work. Did the Lord, then and there, move them to a different dimension in time?

The military members at the base heard and felt the explosion at 10:21, but Pheiffer and staff didn't hear it, feel it, or even know of it, though it happened where they were. It did not touch them or their vehicle.

Pheiffer had been a believer since childhood. One of his staff members had been an atheist, but no longer. He cried out, "This has to be God!"

While Pheiffer was working that day in military intelligence, he had protection not visible.

In the United States he had friends and devout believers who prayed that day for his safety.

May the Lord give us who know Him a calling to be warriors of defense—warriors in prayer.

CHAPTER 10

INTO THE LAND OF GIANTS

Into the promised land the Lord led Israel, by the shortest way, without trespassing on residents. Timidly, the nation sent spies across the Jordan River to report before all the Israelites went into the land of promise. All but two of the spies, Joshua and Caleb, reported:

> "We be not able to go up against the people; for they are stronger than we." And they brought up an evil report of the land which they had searched unto the children of Israel, saying, "The land, through which we have gone to search it, is a land that eateth up the inhabitants thereof; and all the people that we saw in it are men of a great stature. And there we saw giants, the sons of Anak, which come of the giants: and we were in our own sight as grasshoppers, and so we were in their sight." (Num. 13:31–33)

The nation accepted the bad report. They decided to return to Egypt and slavery. They took up stones to stone to death Moses, Aaron, Joshua, and Caleb. The Lord intervened, and His glory appeared in the tabernacle. The sin of the nation was a sin unto death. Moses interceded with prayer. The Lord spared their lives but said:

> "Your carcases shall fall in this wilderness; and all that were numbered of you, according to your whole number, from twenty years old and upward, which have murmured against me, Doubtless ye shall not come into the land, concerning which I sware to make you dwell therein, save Caleb, the son of Jephunneh, and Joshua the son of Nun. But your little ones, which ye said should be a prey, them will I bring in, and they shall know the land which ye have despised. But as for you, your carcases, they shall fall in this wilderness. And your children shall wander in the wilderness forty years, and bear your whoredoms, until your carcases be wasted in the wilderness." (Num. 14:29–33)

The nation wandered in the wilderness until the time of judgment passed. Joshua and Caleb remained in health. The time to enter the promised land had come.

The Lord spoke to Joshua, appointing him to lead Israel over the Jordan River, into the land "flowing with milk and honey"; a fertile land of springs and pastures, but a land of walled cities defended by fierce tribes and even a race of giant humans. The Lord reminded Joshua of the boundaries of the promised land, just as He had told Abraham and Moses:

"Every place that the sole of your foot shall tread upon, that have I given unto you, as I said unto Moses. From the wilderness and this Lebanon even unto the great river, the river Euphrates, all the land of the Hitites, and unto the great sea toward the going down of the sun, shall be your coast. There shall not any man be able to stand before thee all the days of thy life: as I was with Moses, so I will be with thee: I will not fail thee, nor forsake thee." (Josh. 1:3–5)

It was a time of the Jordan's flood, yet the priests bearing the ark went into the river on dry ground, for scripture tells us:

The waters which come down from above stood and rose up upon an heap … and the priests that bare the ark of the covenant of the Lord stood firm on dry ground in the midst of Jordan and all the Israelites passed over on dry ground until all the people were passed clear over Jordan. (Josh. 3:16–17)

The Lord spoke to Joshua of a memorial. Twelve stones were placed in the center of the river where they had passed over, and twelve stones in a heap at the place of their lodging after crossing. A stone represented each tribe of the nation.

A new day had dawned. Israel was in the promised land, but it had to be occupied.

It is said that the Jordan River represents death. True enough, this river represents death and, as Paul told believers, our reckoning ourselves dead to sin; and the promised land represents living in the power of Christ's resurrection:

> Knowing that Christ being raised from the dead
> dieth no more; death hath no more dominion over
> him. For in that he died, he died unto sin once:
> but in that he liveth, he liveth unto God. Likewise
> reckon ye also yourselves to be dead indeed unto sin,
> but alive unto God through Jesus Christ our Lord.
> (Rom. 6:9–11)

The promised land was a land occupied by the enemy of Israel. It was the place of warfare by conquest. As believers, we still encounter walled cities of Satan's domain: bad habits and ways of thinking in our own characters. The Lord wants us to have victory over these and thereby fulfill His plan for our lives. This is the discipleship that the Bible invokes. It is the cross looked at from the perspective of the believer. Jordan is the cross applied to our daily lives—the land of promise—whereas the Red Sea is the cross looked at from the one who is just entering the kingdom of God. It, too, must be kept in memory. Regrettably, I think many professors of religion spend their lives wandering in the wilderness, never fulfilling the plan the Lord must have for them.

The unbeliever, to be saved, looks at the cross, saying, "Christ died for our sins," believing it to be so and never forgetting it. The believer, after salvation, looks at the cross as the obligation and privilege of discipleship, as Jesus said:

> And when he had called the people unto him with
> his disciples also, he said unto them, "Whosoever
> will come after me, let him deny himself, and take
> up his cross, and follow me. For whosoever will save
> his life shall lose it; but whosoever shall lose his life

for my sake and the gospel's, the same shall save it."
(Mark 8:34–35)

The example of Israel's crossing the Jordan provides a lesson for us, if we would follow the Lord Jesus in the plan and promise He has for our lives. First of all, we must have faith in Christ. The ones who did not enter the promised land, instead dying in the wilderness, died "because of unbelief." Here is one of the greatest tragedies ever recorded. They had the faith to cross the Red Sea but not the faith to enter the promised land. An interesting point. The scripture tells us Moses kept the Passover "by faith." The nation as a whole kept its ritual, but the scripture makes no mention they kept it by faith. The Passover, as we have seen, portrays Christ's blood shed for our sins and believed. The promised land is for believers only. As the apostle John says, "they went out from us, but they were not of us, for if they had been of us, they would no doubt have continued with us; but they went out, that they might be manifest that they were not of us" (1 John 2:19). If a person is religious but has no faith in the Lord Jesus Christ, the lifesaving blessing that can come is for such a person to find that out. The surgeon who points out the terminal cancer at a time it can be completely removed saves the patient's life. There are checkpoints in the scripture; these tests show whether a person has the life of Christ within that comes with the new birth by faith in Christ. Herein the Israelites failed the most obvious of tests: they did not continue in the faith; they turned back.

The Lord promised Abraham, Moses, and Joshua the land bounded by the Mediterranean Sea (the great sea) all the way to the Euphrates River. Joshua led the nation in great success, taking the walled cities even where giant human creatures lived, but he and Israel took but a small portion of the land of promise. Their conquest was bounded, for the most part, by the Jordan River, far from the Euphrates River.

Our grant (as disciples) is to be like Him, our Lord and Leader. Someday "at His coming," we shall, as the apostle John tells us, be like Him, "see Him as He is" when He comes again. In the meantime, we have a long way to go, as Paul says:

> But what things were gain to me, those I counted loss for Christ. Yea doubtless, and I count all things but loss for the excellency of the knowledge of Christ Jesus my Lord: for whom I have suffered the loss of all things, and do count them but dung, that I may win Christ, And be found in him, not having mine own righteousness, which is of the law, but that which is through the faith of Christ, the righteousness which is of God by faith: That I may know him, and the power of his resurrection, and the fellowship of his sufferings, being made comformable unto his death; If by any means I might attain unto the resurrection of the dead. Not as though I had already attained, either were already perfect; but I follow after, if that I may apprehend that for which also I am apprehended of Christ Jesus. Brethren, I count not myself to have apprehended: but this one thing I do, forgetting those things which are behind, and reaching forth unto those things which are before, I press toward the mark for the prize of the high calling of God in Christ Jesus. (Phil. 3:7–14)

The experience of discipleship—following Jesus—has many rewards: the power to witness; the power to walk in the Spirit, in fellowship with the Son of God Himself; joy in trial and suffering; power in prayer; the power, through the Spirit, to walk by faith above all the old habits of sin; fellowship with other disciples. These are but a few of the many rewards.

But know this: The path of discipleship, though continual, must be entered. Jesus set the requirement—one must take up his cross and follow Him. When Israel entered, finally, the land of promise, they again kept the Passover. The gospel that is the power of salvation to all who believe must never be forgotten. But no longer did they eat manna; rather, they ate the produce of the new land. No more water from a rock that followed them. They watered themselves and their flocks from the flowing waters in Canaan.

Knowing and following the will of God, the very place where He wants you and me, is rich with spiritual food and drink. How to know the will of God for one's life? God's Word gives the answer in plain terms: "I beseech you therefore, brethren, by the mercies of God, that ye present your bodies a living sacrifice, holy, acceptable unto God, which is your reasonable service" (Rom. 12:1). Notice the appeal is to saved people, "brethren." This appeal is based on the previous passages in Romans, justification by faith.

"Present your bodies a living sacrifice" is not just advice or a doctrine. It is an act of faith. It is the "take up your cross" of Jesus's invitation. The very same word is used here as when

Mary and Joseph brought the baby Jesus to the temple "to present Him to the Lord." The walk of discipleship can be continuous, but it must have a beginning. As has been said, "When we are saved we have all of Christ but He does not have all of us." Discipleship is giving all of ourselves to Him. It can begin immediately after the new birth, just as the Feast of Unleavened Bread began on the fifteenth of Nisan (this is the first month of the Jewish religious calendar), immediately after Passover.

The apostle Paul said to believers:

> Purge out therefore the old leaven, that ye may be a new lump, as ye are unleavened. For even Christ our Passover is sacrificed for us: Therefore let us keep the feast, not with old leaven, neither with the leaven of malice and wickedness; but with the unleavened bread of sincerity and truth. (1 Cor. 5:7–8)

Seems a contradiction, doesn't it? Telling his church they are unleavened, then telling them to purge out their old leaven (sin). But it is not a contradiction. The moment we are saved, we are "complete in Him." The land of promise is ours. But we have a long way to go and many walled cities to conquer before we make it ours by possession in our lives. In the meantime, we can take satisfaction in this: "But of him are ye in Christ Jesus, who of God is made unto us wisdom, and righteousness, and sanctification, and redemption: That, according as it is written, He that glorieth, let him glory in the Lord" (1 Cor. 1:30–31).

Any who have never received Christ by faith need to go through that door of new birth by faith before venturing on discipleship. Otherwise, it is a path to disappointment. All of Christ's apostles were born again, having "beheld the lamb of God that taketh away the sin of the world" under the ministry of John the Baptist before Jesus called them into discipleship.

One does not attempt to take up the will of a neighbor who passed away, trying to claim rights to the property the will grants to the neighbor's children. Yet unbelievers—and many of them—try to make the scriptures directed to, and with promises to, believers as also to unbelievers. They are like a maid who picks up and reads a letter written not to her, but to her mistress, from her mistress's husband, that reads, "Dear wife, when I return I will take you on a trip for a second honeymoon to a beautiful resort I have discovered." The maid then meets the husband at the door when he returns, saying, "I am ready to go to the resort, dear." She is going to be disappointed.

I am convinced there are not just a few in the church who testify that their salvation was when they gave their lives to Christ, when the truth is that, growing up in a Christian home and hearing the gospel, they, at a very early age, feeling their wrongfulness, received the Lord by faith. They were saved then and there, and they began a renewed discipleship later, when they gave their lives to the Lord. "But Jesus said, Suffer little children, and forbid them not, to come unto me: for of such is the kingdom of heaven" (Matt. 19:14).

In a sense, they were correct in their testimony, as has often been said, "We were, when we first believed, saved from the penalty of sin. We are being saved from the power of sin. When Jesus returns we shall be saved from the presence of sin." These statements are quite true, I think.

Some churches delay baptism of small children until they can understand the full meaning of baptism and discipleship. It is not that these children are not saved—fully and eternally saved—the moment they first received the Lord, because they are. Rather, they are baptized later to establish and confirm them on the road of discipleship. Children who are saved and discipled at an early age become, in many cases, the deacons, the Sunday school teachers, and the pastors of churches. Where would we be without them? They have not so many giants occupying walled cities to bring down and occupy as those of us who begin on the road to glory at a later age.

The apostle Paul tells us:

> For though we walk in the flesh, we do not war after the flesh: (for the weapons of our warfare are not carnal, but mighty through God to the pulling down of strong holds;) Casting down imaginations, and every high thing that exalteth itself against the knowledge of God, and bringing into captivity every thought to the obedience of Christ. (2 Cor. 10:3–5)

These weapons, (the sword of the Spirit, which is the Word of God, exercised in prayer), are powerful within ourselves and without, in life's battles, to take to ourselves that which is according to the will of God in the property of His promise.

To illustrate, I offer a true example from my own experience. I hesitate to give it for fear some will use it to emulate, looking to another's actual experience rather than to Christ. Nevertheless, with the caveat to not emulate others instead of looking to our Lord, I proceed.

From early childhood, I had within me—in my heart, as we would say—a feeling of anger. It was like a hot ember. At times it would flame out in fury. "Bad temper," people said. It continued as an adult. I learned to control it to some extent so that it did not damage professionally or socially, but at home it hurt others at times. One morning, I read from Luther's *Commentary on Galatians,* his exposition of chapter 2, verse 20, the following words:

> Paul speaketh, not here of crucifying by imitation or example (for to follow the example of Christ is also to be crucified with Him) which crucifying belongeth to the flesh. "Christ suffered for us, leaving us an example that ye should follow His steps." But he speaketh of that high crucifying, whereby sin, the devil, and death are crucified in Christ and not in me. Here Christ Jesus doth all Himself alone. But I believing in Christ, am by faith crucified also with Christ, so that all these things are crucified and dead unto me.

> "Nevertheless I live." I speak not so, saith he, of my death and crucifying, as though I now lived not: yeah, I live, for I am quickened by this death

and crucifying, through the which I die: that is, forasmuch as I am delivered from the law, sin, and death, I now live indeed. Wherefore that crucifying, and that death, whereby I am crucified and dead to the law, sin, death, and all evils, is to me resurrection and life. For Christ crucified the devil, He killed death, condemned sin, and bound the law; and I believing this, am delivered from the law, sin, death, and the devil.

Here (as I have said before) we must observe Paul's manner of speaking. He saith that we are dead and crucified to the law, whereas in very deed the law itself is dead and crucified unto us. But this manner of speech he useth here of purpose, that it may be the more sweet and comfortable unto us. For the law (which notwithstanding continueth, liveth and reigneth in the whole world, which also accuseth and condemneth all men) is crucified and dead unto those only which believe in Christ: therefore to them alone belongeth this glory, that they are dead to sin, hell, death, and the devil.

I prayed, placing myself with Christ in His death and resurrection. I spoke to the Lord, as in Romans, chapter 12, verse 1, and said, "Here is my body an offering." And I felt the feeling of anger, with me from childhood, go out of me like a breath. This feeling has stayed out, and the hot ember bothers me no more.

Our weapons of warfare are powerful on matters concerning others as well. An illustration: There was a psychologist with a high permanent civil-service rating who met a catastrophe. The attorney general of his state gave an opinion that his position required a license, which he did not have. A permanent position in civil service is usually secure. The job is safe, but not if the position is abolished. That is what happened. The department head dismissed the psychologist because his position was abolished. Usually, the employee will be transferred to another department of like status, if available, but in this case, transfer to another department was not available. Because of a decrease in tax revenue, the governing body had declared a freeze on adding employees to any department. The psychologist secured a lawyer and appealed the decision to the personnel board. The lawyer went to trial on the case, with the dim hope of the personnel board recommending the psychologist be kept on the payroll in the position as a nonprofessional helper, since the psychologist had a good record; and within a year, he could take the required test and secure the mandated license.

Now, a word here about state administrative trials. The tryors of fact are an uneven number of officers. Proceedings are, in some ways, similar to trials in military courts-martial. The tryors of fact are also the tryors of law (the place of a judge), but there is a lawyer who sits with the officers to advise on the law. All proceedings are taken down by a court reporter. There is a clerk present to take filings and produce records, and a lawyer is there to represent the state.

There is an obvious difference, however, from a jury trial. The officers hearing the evidence as tryors of fact, unlike a jury, can, through the presiding officer, ask the parties questions and even make comments. In this way, parties to the case can often tell which way the case is going, win or lose.

Now, to the proceeding at hand. After a day of trial: the notice of job termination to the psychologist, the opinions of the attorney general, and the psychologist's record of employment were all in evidence. The good character and job performance of the psychologist, by witnesses, were also in evidence; but a bad direction of the case became obvious. Because of the comments and questions of the officers hearing the matter, it became obvious that the job termination was to be affirmed and the psychologist dismissed from employment. Then, trial was ordered recessed until the following day.

The lawyer suddenly awakened early that next morning, and words came to his mind: *Attack the attorney general's opinion.* The lawyer thought to himself, *How foolish; government bodies always, always follow the attorney general's opinions—but we are losing anyway, and adding foolishness to it cannot make us lose any more.*

On the lawyer's behalf and unkown to him, the psychologist's friends had spent time in prayer the night before, exercising the sword of the Spirit:

> Verily I say unto you, Whatsoever ye shall bind on earth shall be bound in heaven: and whatsoever ye shall loose on earth shall be loosed in heaven. Again I say unto you, That if two of you shall agree on earth as touching anything that they shall ask, it shall be done for them of my Father which is in heaven. (Matt. 18:18–19)

Recess over, the trial began. The lawyer introduced in evidence a large chart, and on it a previous state statute he claimed voided the attorney general's opinion. Then, the lawyer asked, as a sworn witness, the department head that had ordered the psychologist's dismissal from his job, "If it had not been for the attorney general's opinion, would you have fired him?" The department head remained silent. The lawyer repeated the question over and over. The department head finally replied, "No, I would not have fired him."

The lawyer turned and said to the officials, "I move the dismissal of this psychologist be voided, and he be reinstated with all benefits of office, including health insurance, retirement benefits, and back pay restored." The hearing officials turned to their lawyer for advice. Their counselor said, "He is right; the opinion of the attorney general is wrong." The Lord had intervened! The hearing officials, in written decision, voided the dismissal and returned the psychologist to his position, with all benefits and back pay. And he continued in his job until retirement.

The scriptures tell us, "Ye have not because ye ask not." The weapons of our warfare are mighty to the pulling down of strongholds. One cannot overestimate the power of prayer. When we walk with the Lord, "whatever we ask, we receive of him, because we keep his commandments, and do those things that are pleasing in his sight" (1 John 3:22). Much happens because believers pray. Much doesn't happen because believers don't pray.

To illustrate: Two friends continued their friendship for more than thirty years and then even after one became infirm. They spent many days in the outdoors on camping trips. They played golf during the week. They, with their wives, attended church and social functions weekly. Now, this is the interesting point. In all the years of their friendship not one of them asked the other for anything that was denied. Yes, they made many requests of each other, but always within knowledge of the other's interest and ability.

One cannot have a friend unless interests are common and shared. As the scripture says, "Can two walk together except they be agreed?" (Amos 3:3). When we walk with the Lord, our interests are shared, and our requests are granted.

Many of us have had spiritual enemies, habits, fears, and ways of wrong thinking. They, like giants, occupy our lives on territory Christ, the Testator, gave us in His will. (Heb. 9:14–16)

The usurper, Satan, presses the battle in the mind, as the snake poisonous even with its head crushed. Remember he is a defeated foe.

We know that victory on the battleground with Satan, as elsewhere in spiritual concerns, is by faith. But here is where the wheels of progress slow down and sometimes grind to a halt because we have little faith when an issue is before us.

There is a faith builder that helps when it is used in time of trial. This faith builder is remembrance of past successes wrought for us by God.

Drawing from the savings bank of memories of previous struggles and, by faith, with victories, is drawing on a bank whose funds cannot deplete. In fact, the more you use it, the more it grows. (Compare Mark 8:16–20.)

An example: The wonderful story of how, in war, David, with a sling and five stones, killed Goliath, a giant who was trained for personal combat from childhood. Goliath's spear had a shaft like a weaver's beam. He had a helper who went with him, carrying a body shield in his front so that he could use both hands and arms in combat.

The outcome of the battle between Goliath and the youth David was of major consequence. Each represented his respective country. To the winner went the reward of his nation's hope.

Goliath's Philistines coveted Israel's land. They wanted to keep it. David's Israel wanted possession of the same land. It was theirs. The Lord had given it to them.

In their meeting, David ran toward Goliath, with visible armament of only a sling and five stones. But David had a more powerful weapon: faith in God's help, buttressed by the memory of previous battles.

When David had volunteered to his king, Saul, for combat with Goliath, he gave testimony to these past victories (1 Sam. 17:34–36): victories in a mortal conflict with a lion and a bear attempting to raid David's flock.

In the conflict with Goliath, David brought him down—only one stone to the giant's forehead, and then cut off his head with the giant's own sword. There were four more stones in reserve.

What happened to Goliath's shield bearer, we don't know. Likely, he ran away. Israel had possession of their land because their champion had defeated the giant.

Earlier, Samuel, Israel's prophet and judge who had anointed David to be king, set an example. Israel won a victory in battle with the Philistines; then Samuel placed a stone he named Ebenezer. It was a monument for remembrance, on the very place the battle was won.

Samuel said, "Hitherto hath the Lord helped us" (1 Sam. 7:12).

Have we not, with God's help, overcome dangers past? Then, let us take the memory of one similar to the trial we now face, and keep it in mind. May God grant us to place in the armory of our soul victorious stones of remembrance so that we, by faith, can use them to occupy the territory willed us by our Savior.

CHAPTER 11

REST FOR THE TRAVELER

We meet enemies on the road to heaven. Their objective is to block our path and make us lose our way. Some enemies are apparent. Some are clothed in deceit. Knowing this, we need to have our present standing before God settled, so that we may take with confidence the armament He has provided (Eph. 6:13–18). This confidence, a rest in our relationship with God, allows us to move on in the way before us—its battles and the celebration of its victories. How very vulnerable we are to attack and the temptation to turn back if we are not resting, secure, in God's promises that we are His. The scripture tells us, "There remaineth therefore a rest to the people of God" (Heb. 4:9).

Rest is a word that speaks of the refreshment and satisfaction experienced upon the completion of a project; the relief from the burden of labor it has entailed. The believer's rest in faith is compared to the rest God took after completing the creation of the world, with its humans, Adam and Eve, in His own image. He found it very good (Gen. 1:31).

The prophetic word has a future fulfillment. Often, it also has a present application. "There remaineth therefore a rest to the people of God," is herein in keeping with the theme of this text, applied to our present life of faith.

Today, the Lord Jesus leads His people into rest. Rest from the burdens of an accusing conscience; rest from any obligation to keep all of God's law; rest from trying to be acceptable to God by our good works; rest from a vain, futile attempt at self-fulfillment. Truly, "For we which have believed do enter into rest ..." (Heb. 4:3).

With the good news comes a responsibility. "Let us therefore fear, lest, a promise being left us of entering into his rest, any of you should seem to come short of it" (Heb. 4:1).

Comparing our lot in life with that of the people of Israel while serving Pharaoh in Egypt, we see that we all are born into this world with struggles to bear. Soon the rules of right and wrong bind us in the doing of wrong, inwardly if not outwardly. Some parents teach their children the law of Moses, centered on the Ten Commandments. Others simply give rules of conduct, whatever they may be, whether under written law or the works of the law written in the conscience. Regardless, eventually, we find ourselves law breakers, inwardly and often outwardly. Soon we find ourselves bound by ways of thinking and doing that enslave us. As the scripture says, "Jesus answered them, Verily, verily, I say unto you, whosoever committeth sin is the servant of sin" (John 8:34). The rules of conduct learned in our conscience condemn us, but relief is promised. Jesus says, "come unto me and I will give you rest."

The scripture says, "Today if ye will hear his voice, Harden not your hearts, as in the provocation, in the day of temptation in the wilderness" (Heb. 3:7–8).

The early Christians, most of them Jews, faced the temptation to return to Judaism. We face the temptation, when trials come, to turn back from our faith and look to our old ways. The Israelites who failed to go into the promised land under Moses failed because they feared adversaries dangerous to their occupation. Next they left off resting in God's promise and looked to their own works as necessary to get to the promised land. The exhortation in the scripture is to us, as believers, to continue in faith. "But Christ as a son over his own house; whose house are we, if we hold fast the confidence and the rejoicing of the hope firm unto the end" (Heb. 3:6). Thank God, He keeps us " ... preserved in Jesus Christ, and called:" (Jude 1:1).

The rest from our works to be acceptable to God is a rest in Christ. It must be diligently pursued! (Heb. 4:11) Satan and our flesh tempt us to leave off looking at the finished work of God in Christ's crucifixion and resurrection. When Christ ascended afterward into heaven he "sat down" on the right hand of God. The work of eternal salvation is finished, and it is done entirely by God, not us. We enter into it by faith. Good works follow. (Heb. 11)

One Christian scholar comments on the foregoing in this way:

> The salvation which the writer has previously referred to as a glorious dominion is here spoken of as a Rest. The significance lies in its being God's rest which man is to share. It is the rest which God has enjoyed since the creation. From all His creative work, God could not be said to rest until, after what cannot but appear to us a million of hazards, man appeared. He was a creature in whose history God Himself could find a worthy history; whose moral and spiritual needs would elicit the Divine resources and exercise what is deepest in God. When man appears, God is satisfied, for here is one in His own image. But from this bare statement of the meaning of God's rest, it is obvious that God's people must share it with Him. God's rest is satisfaction with man; but this satisfaction can be perfected only when man is in perfect harmony with Him. His rest is not perfect until they rest in Him.[7]

The scripture compares the rest we have to the Sabbath day. We seldom appreciate the strict application of this law of Moses. In Numbers 15:32, there is the record of a man who gathered sticks on the Sabbath day. Was he gathering for a fire to warm himself

---

[7] From Marcus Dods, *The Expositors' Greek Testament*, vol. 4, ed. W. Robertson Nicoll (Grand Rapids, MI: Eerdmans Publishing Company, 1980), 280–81.

or to cook on? We don't know. Perhaps he was just cleaning up the ground in front of his tent. The Israelites brought this man to Moses and the congregation. They put him in custody until judgment was passed. Note this: "The Lord said unto Moses, the man shall be surely put to death: All the congregation shall stone him with stones without the camp" (Num. 15:35). They "brought him without the camp, and stoned him with stones, and he died; as the Lord commanded Moses."

Sound severe? It certainly does, and it's in the scriptures for a purpose: to show us the necessity to be in God's kingdom, with our inheritance, by faith alone. There remaineth "a rest to the people of God" (Heb. 4:9). We are to keep on resting in Christ. We walk by faith. We reach our heavenly city by faith.

Martin Luther describes this Sabbath rest of faith as follows, in his commentary on Galatians:

> For in the righteousness of faith, we work nothing, we render nothing unto God, but we only receive, and suffer another to work in us, that is to say, God. Therefore, it seemeth good unto us to call this righteousness of faith, the passive righteousness. This is a righteousness hidden in a mystery, which the world doth not know, yea, Christians themselves do not thoroughly understand it, and can hardly take hold of it in their temptations. Therefore, it must be diligently taught, and continually practiced. And whoso doth not understand or apprehend this righteousness, in afflictions and terrors of conscience, must needs be overthrown. For there is

no comfort of conscience so firm and sure, as this passive righteousness.[8]

The spearhead of the Reformation was Luther's teaching on justification by faith alone.

This faith is entirely contrary to our own way and nature. We come into this world "working at it." We work and struggle to make our way in life. As to our salvation from sin, it is entirely different. "To him that worketh not but believeth on Him that justifieth the ungodly, his faith is counted for righteousness" (Rom. 4:5).

A frequent criticism calls this doctrine "easy believism." To such, I say, "If it is so easy, why don't you try it?" It is not easy. It is impossible, unless God works in our hearts. "Faith and that not of yourselves: it is the gift of God: Not of works, lest any man should boast" (Eph. 2:8–9).

Some of the most meaningful words ever spoken show the grounds for this rest of faith. In the Gospel of Matthew, concerning the death of Christ on the cross, we read, "Jesus when he had cried again with a loud voice yielded up the ghost" (Matt. 27:50). In the Gospel of John, we find out what Jesus said when He cried with a loud voice; this, no doubt, was for public record, as when He raised Lazarus, Jesus also shouted with a loud voice. He said, "It is finished" (*tetelestai*) (John 19:30). *Tetelestai*, translated "it is finished," was a word used in commercial transactions. It had a meaning similar to "paid in

---

[8] Martin Luther, *Commentary on Galatians*, xii–xiii.

full" written on a receipt today. The long overdue debt mankind owed for a violation of God's law was finished—"paid in full"— the work of redemption prophesied, set forth in foreshadow and sacrifices accomplished, finished; the long-awaited promise of the Seed of the woman to bruise the head of the serpent (Satan) finished, accomplished; the curse of the law showing man's duty but giving him no power to do it, finished. "Blotting out the handwriting of ordinances that was against us, which was contrary to us, and took it out of the way, nailing it to his cross; And having spoiled principalities and powers, he made a shew of them openly, triumphing over them in it" (Col. 2:14–15). And Christ did it for the believer "once and for all" (Heb. 10:10). Praise God forever!

We often hear this question: "But what about works?" When we believe, God creates us unto good works from above, by faith; the Holy Spirit places love in our hearts, a love that fulfills the law. When we love our fellow man, we do not steal from him. When he is in need, we help him and so fulfill God's commandment to us: "And this is his commandment, that we should believe on the name of his Son Jesus Christ, and love one another, as he gave us commandment" (1 John. 3:23).

As Luther pointedly puts it:

> Paul saith, "I live, yet not I, but Christ liveth in me," he speaketh, as it were, in his own person. Therefore, he correcteth himself in the second part of the sentence, saying: "Yet not I." That is I live not now in my own person, but Christ liveth in me. Indeed the person liveth, but not in himself,

nor for anything that is in him. But who is that I, of whom he saith, "yet not I?" This I is he which hath the law, and is bound to do the works thereof: who also is a person separate from Christ. This person Paul rejecteth. For he is separate from Christ, he belongeth to death and hell. Therefore he saith: "Not I but Christ liveth in me." He is my form, my furniture and perfection, adorning and beautifying my faith, as the colour, the clear light, or the whiteness do garnish and beautify the wall. Thus are we constrained grossly to set forth this matter. For we cannot spiritually conceive that Christ is so nearly joined and united unto us, as the colour or whiteness are to this wall. Christ therefore, saith he, thus joined and united unto me, and abiding in me, liveth this life in me which now I live; yea Christ Himself is this life, which not I live. Wherefore Christ and I in this behalf are both one. This union or conjunction, then, is the cause that I am delivered from the terror of the law and sin, am separate from myself, and translated unto Christ and His Kingdom, which is a kingdom of grace, righteousness, peace, joy, life, salvation, and eternal glory. Whilst I thus abide and dwell in Him, what evil is there that can hurt me?[9]

---

[9] Martin Luther, *Commentary on Galatians,* 88–89.

CHAPTER 12

THE ROAD TO GLORY

It has been said of the Bible that in the Old Testament we have the New Testament concealed, and in the New Testament we have the Old Testament revealed.

We will now fast-forward nearly fifteen hundred years, from the days of Joshua and ancient Israel in their taking part of the promised land in Canaan, to a prominent event in the lives of His apostles, Peter, James, and John, in the time when Christ was on earth. It was in the same land and some months before He was crucified.

Jesus said to them:

"But I tell you of a truth, there be some standing here, which shall not taste of death, till they see the kingdom of God." And it came to pass about an eight days after these sayings, he took Peter and John and James, and went up into a mountain to pray. And as he prayed, the fashion of his countenance was altered, and his raiment was white and glistering. And, behold, there talked with him two men, which were Moses and Elias:[10] Who appeared in glory, and spake of his decease, which he should accomplish at Jerusalem. (Luke 9:27–31)

Moses, whom the Lord buried in an unknown place, represents those believers who have passed away, and Elijah represents those who are alive when the Lord returns.

Here is the promise of the believer's future and the glory of God:

For the Lord himself shall descend from heaven with a shout, with the voice of the archangel, and with the trump of God: and the dead in Christ shall rise first: Then we which are alive and remain shall be caught up together with them in the clouds, to meet the Lord in the air: and so shall we ever be with the Lord. (1 Thess. 4:16–17)

We believers will be with Him on the road to the city whose builder and maker is God. We believers are on the road of glory, to the resurrection of our earthly bodies to bodies fashioned like His glorious body. Christ is the firstfruits of the resurrection.

---

[10] The person here, named Elias (a translation from the Greek, the original language of the New Testament scriptures), is the same person as the one named Elijah in the Old Testament, the original language of which is Hebrew; hence the slight difference in the spelling of the name.

We who believe will be like Him, made so "in a twinkling of an eye," at His return to a new and glorious dimension—a miracle.

We don't fully understand how a wormlike creature in the sediment at the bottom of a river can be changed from one form to another, and emerge into the air a shimmering mayfly with iridescent wings, even though such events are purely earthly and happen countless times each year in North America and Europe.

The mystery of the resurrection is a spiritual matter, as is the new birth into God's kingdom, which we experience by faith.

The Word tells us the "dead in Christ shall rise first." Wherever our bodies are—buried or not buried—and at whatever time, the Lord who buried Moses knows. A great miracle He performed when He was on earth was the resurrection of Lazarus:

> Jesus said, "Take ye away the stone." Martha, the sister of him that was dead, saith unto him, "Lord, by this time he stinketh: for he hath been dead four days." Jesus saith unto her, "Said I not unto thee, that, if thou wouldest believe, though shouldest see the glory of God?" Then they took away the stone from the place where the dead was laid. And Jesus lifted up his eyes, and said, "Father, I thank thee that thou hast heard me. And I knew that thou hearest me always: but because of the people which stand by I said It, that they may believe that thou has sent me." And when he thus had spoken, he cried with a loud voice, "Lazarus, come forth." And he that was dead came forth, bound hand and foot with grave-clothes: and his face was bound about

with a napkin. Jesus saith unto them, "Loose him,
and let him go." (John 11:39–44)

Lazarus, dead four days, his soul and spirit in paradise away
from his body, presents in his resurrection a picture of the
power of Christ over death. His body, Martha said, "Stinketh."
Some of it had gone in gases. Some had been taken in by the
creatures of decay, and yet, Lazarus came out when the Lord
called him, whole as he had been when he went in. Jesus said,
"I am alpha and omega, the beginning and the ending" (Rev.
1:8)—not "I will be the ending," but "I am the ending." He is
present in time and outside time.

Einstein is famous for, among other things, defining the fourth
dimension: where something is in time. Jesus is Lord of the
fourth dimension. He is the great I Am.

William Tyndale translated the Bible from Hebrew and Greek
into our English language. The King James Version is based, in
great part, on the Tyndale translation. When Tyndale translated
the Bible, it was a crime to do so. Religious authorities captured
Tyndale, tried him, and burned him at the stake. Then, to
deny him resurrection, they took his ashes and scattered them
in the ocean. No matter. The great I Am knew and knows,
and when the trumpet sounds, the same body of Tyndale that
burned at the stake will come out, alive, joined with his soul
and spirit, but with the glorious body no longer affected by
death and decay, fashioned after the body the Lord Jesus now
has in heaven. "We shall be like Him," and we shall be "ever
with the Lord."

Moses was dead. God had buried him. But, when the disciples saw him, clothed in the brightest white, talking with the Lord nearly fifteen hundred years later, he was alive and well.

Job prophesied this beautiful future, the glory to which we believers are headed:

> "For I know that my redeemer liveth, and that he shall stand at the latter day upon the earth: And though after my skin, worms destroy this body, yet in my flesh shall I see God: Whom I shall see for myself, and mine eyes shall behold, and not another; though my reins be consumed within me." (Job 19:25–27)

Elijah, on the Mount of Transfiguration, represents those of us who are alive when the Lord returns and, like those who have passed away, hear the trumpet and the call of the Lord, are transfigured into glorious bodies in the resurrection, and meet the Lord in the air. You remember that Elijah went to heaven in a chariot of fire, without dying (2 Kings 2:11).

In the scripture, the Lord's coming is compared to different figures. His coming unexpectedly, at any time, is like a thief in the night (Matt. 24:43–44). He is coming to take up His own people, and then, later, with His own, He is coming back to earth, "when every eye shall see Him"; as the angels said, "Ye men of Galilee, why stand ye gazing up into heaven? This same Jesus, which is taken up from you into heaven, shall so come in like manner as ye have seen him go into heaven" (Acts 1:11). (See Matt. 24:27; Matt. 24:30; Rev. 19:13-16).

His coming for His own was prophesied in poetry, in the Old Testament; His people who are caught up are compared to a bride taken by the bridegroom:

> The voice of my beloved! Behold, he cometh leaping upon the mountains, skipping upon the hills. My beloved is like a roe or a young hart: behold, he standeth behind our wall, he looketh forth at the windows, shewing himself through the lattice. My beloved spake, and said unto me, "Rise up, my love, my fair one, and come away. For, lo, the winter is past, the rain is over and gone." (Song of Sol. 2:8–11)

His coming is also compared to one making up his precious jewels and to be spared the judgment He will bring on the earth when and after He appears with His people:

> "And they shall be mine, saith the Lord of hosts, in that day when I make up my jewels; and I will spare them as a man spareth his own son that serveth him. Then shall ye return, and discern between the righteous and the wicked, between him that serveth God and him that serveth him not" (Mal. 3:17–18)

And those who are not ready are like the foolish attendants to a bride who were to go in celebration of the marriage, with lamps burning. They took no oil. Their lamps wouldn't burn, and while they went to buy oil, the bridegroom came, and they were left out (Matt. 25:1–13). One cannot buy oil in the middle of the night for use in this lamp. Their efforts were futile. The oil is provided by the bridegroom with the wedding feast, as was the custom at the time. The oil isn't for sale. The oil typifies the Holy Spirit, which is given freely by the

Bridegroom—Christ—to all who believe. They who have not the Spirit are none of His (Rom. 8:9).

As to His coming for His own, there are no signs. He simply says, "Watch." We do not and will not know when the trumpet will sound and those who have died in the Lord go first and we who are alive are caught up together with them in the air. A blink of the eye, and it is over. It could have happened at any time after or even during the apostolic age. It will be like a thief in the night. It could happen before you read this sentence. When God's people are taken out of this world, think of the misery that will follow. The salt that keeps it from rotting will be gone. The light that shows the way, even proper conduct, will be gone. Judgment follows. The Four Horsemen of the book of Revelation, anti-Christ—war, famine, and death—ride over the earth (Rev. 6:1–8).

Whereas there are no signs as to His coming for His people, signs are given us as to His coming later, with His people, including the rebirth of the nation of Israel, the fig tree (Matt. 24:32–34). (Additionally, see Song of Sol. 2:13.)

When He comes, He will judge the nations, and Israel will accept Him; in fact, the whole world will turn to Him: "For the earth shall be filled with the knowledge of the glory of the Lord, as the waters cover the sea" (Hab. 2:14).

At times, the Lord, even now, gives us a picture of the time when this world will be converted to Christ. We see it in the book of Acts, in chapter 8. Philip, a missionary, went to the city of Samaria, and the people "with one accord gave heed unto those things which Phillip spake."

Now, there are few who are interested in the gospel, and few who follow Christ. After His coming to earth, what a difference it will be. A reminder of the day to come is in the good result of missionary work that happened recently.

A certain man—we will call him Giver—gave in the form of regular donations to a missionary and his wife in Peru. The missionary gave information that his wife, who grew up in a village at the headwaters of the Amazon River in Peru, near Ecuador, had discovered important events. The national government had built a brick school building for the children. Catholics had provided two nuns—sisters fluent in the local language and Spanish—who could serve as teachers in the school, but there was not a book in the village.

This was a primitive village in the floodplain at the start of the Amazon River. Near the village was a flowing spring of clean water making a small stream, which, at places, was four feet deep. This village was on no road or travel route. Communication was by boat, with the boatman coming every few weeks to a landing three or four miles away, to trade for the plantains the villagers grew and bring them communication from the "outside world."

The villagers were of an ancient but vigorous tribe. In fact, at the beginning of the twentieth century, they were a fearsome tribe of head hunters. Their dialect had never been reduced to writing. Some twenty years before, Bible translators had visited but were unable to translate the native speech into a known language and so gave up trying to interpret any of the dialect. No Caucasians had visited the villagers since the translators left. But God had brought changes.

The missionary's wife knew her people's dialect, as well as Spanish and English. Others from the village had moved out and trained in a missionary station in a nearby village serviced by a bush plane, and they also knew the languages.

The missionary gave this information to Giver, and he hoped for a distribution to the village of books of the New Testament, in Spanish. Giver enlisted his Christian friends to pray for this plan, but it seemed unlikely. The missionary's wife warned Giver. She said, "The cacao growers near the village make cocaine. They sell to drug dealers, and they watch the village. They will kill you. You are six feet tall. The people in the village are, like, five feet tall. You stand out like a tall tree in the woods. The cocaine people will think you are a dangerous gringo spy. They will see you, cut you down—kill you."

Giver prayed with his friends, for blessing and safety; after which he believed the Lord would protect him and the giving out of His Word.

At Giver's expense, the missionary and his wife visited and stayed with her parents and kinfolk in the village. They informed the villagers that Giver was coming with books, copies of God's Word written in the language their children could learn in their new school. The Catholic sisters said, "It is a good translation." The door to spreading God's Word opened!

Giver and his wife, with three hundred copies of a Spanish translation of the New Testament, provided by a friend, flew to Lima, Peru. Giver's wife taught the Bible to women in Lima, and Giver, with his scriptures, flew by bush plane into the jungle and visited the outreach of Christianity at a mission school. Here, the Lord took over, in effect, like a halo.

Giver found in the mission station boxes of the whole Bible, in Spanish. He met a young believer, a student of theology, who had grown up in the village. He had wanted to take the Bibles to the village but had no funds to pay the expenses of travel. Travel was available by chartering a bush plane to fly to the village, to high ground—just long enough for a small one-engine plane to land. Giver and the young theologian made plans and scheduled a flight to the village.

The missionary and his wife told the villagers that Giver was coming with books of God's own Word, and experienced the generosity of the expectant tribe. The natives built, without tools, a sort of tabernacle, the first church building in the village: it was built on posts, a sort of post-and-beam construction with a roof thatched with jungle palms. Woven matting formed the walls that could be lowered or rolled up. The tabernacle would hold nearly two hundred people. The Lord was in charge. It was completed the day before Giver and his young theologian friend flew into the village, in two small planes loaded with New Testaments and Bibles. Of course, Giver knew nothing of the new tabernacle or even if the tribe would accept the Bibles. To his surprise, when he landed, he was met by all who could walk from the village. In procession, he, together with the theologian and the missionary and his wife, followed by the villagers who carried their new Bibles, marched like triumphant celebrants to the tabernacle.

The next day, there was a great assembly at the tabernacle: Giver stood in front to speak. The missionary's wife stood beside him to translate the words of Giver, who spoke in short sentences to make it easier for her. He told the villagers the following, much of which they had been told in previous days by the missionary:

"God, the Spirit that created the sun and the moon, did more.

"He created the beautiful forests where you live. He created the water you drink. He created your ancestors, and He created you. You are here in this beautiful building you have made with your hands. Its beauty would be admired by all people in the world if they saw it.

"We are here today, but we have a problem. We know how to do right things. We know some things are wrong. Hating another is wrong. Stealing is wrong. Lying is wrong. Jealousy is wrong. If we have not done these things outwardly, we have done them in our hearts. We all have. Because we do wrong, we will die, and die forever. Because we do wrong, God cannot have fellowship with us. He cannot take us to His home where His people live forever, even after they die. He loved us while we were doing wrong. He sent His only Son to live among us.

His Son was born of a virgin, conceived by the Holy Spirit. His name is Jesus. The books we brought tell you about Him. His Son did no wrong. Wicked men hated Him and killed Him. They nailed Him to a cross. But He let them do it because He loved us, and His death takes our place, so we don't have to die forever. God raised His Son from the grave on the third day. God promises to forgive everyone of all wrongdoing and count His Son's death as the death of all who will believe in Him. That means, believe what I have said about Him taking your place, shedding His blood for you. That means, believing that God raised His Son's body from the grave on the third day, according to this book. That means, this Jesus is alive now, to come into your heart by His Spirit and show you His way.

"Now, all of you will take Jesus in your heart, believing what I have said. Stand up and confess it in this public place."

The missionary, the theologian, Giver, and the interpreter (the missionary's wife) were the only ones standing. Giver thought to himself, *It will be like home. No one will take a stand, but we have put out good seed that may grow anyway.*

To Giver's surprise, immediately upon his last words spoken, everyone—almost the whole village crowded in the tabernacle—stood, rejoicing. After more instruction, the missionary baptized most of the adults of the village, in the adjacent stream.

The rainy season came, and Giver left the village, flying over and through the Andes Mountains, in a bush plane. Time has passed, but Giver feels he will meet again many of those generous and cheerful villagers in heaven. They stepped onto the road to glory.

The door to the road of light and life still has room to enter. Some of the words in the last chapter of the scriptures are words of invitation: "And the Spirit and the bride say, Come. And let him that heareth say, Come. And let him that is athirst come. And whosoever will, let him take the water of life freely" (Rev. 22:17).